FROM THE SHADOW OF INSIGHT

From the Shadow of Insight

by

JOSEPH WANEFSKY

PHILOSOPHICAL LIBRARY
NEW YORK

15 East 40 Street, New York, N. Y. 10016

Library of Congress Catalog Card No. 73-82166
SBN 8022-2128-9

Manufactured in the United States of America

Contents

GENESIS

Chapter 1

The concept that is most essential for the understanding of the Bible is the idea of continuity. The spinal cord of our existence and the central core of our civilization is based upon this idea. G-d attired man in a garment of skin. The question that arises is, why was it necessary for G-d alone to clothe man in a garment of skin. Could not Adam have himself clothed his naked exposure? We read in Genesis that Cain, Abel and Tubal Cain created instruments and built cities. Wouldn't it be simple enough for Adam to clothe himself? G-d alone had to clothe Adam and no one else could have because after Adam's dismal failure in sinning against G-d by eating of the etz hadas he could not extricate himself from the plight, from his spiritual despondency. G-d alone had to elevate man, had to reach out and pluck man from the pitfall of his abyss, from his rapid descending slide into chaos and self-destruction and self-annihilation. This is the paramount example that pervades throughout the entire Bible, that there is a continuity in civilization in the particular civilization of Judaism and in the general world community.

From Israel they declare, she shall no longer fall. Arise, O, then, you betrothed of Israel, from the mire of medieval misery and the misfortune of 2 millenia of exile. The call arises from Judah. Kol omair Karaw.

A voice cries out that Israel shall rejuvenate itself like the burning Phoenix.

Rejuvenate your youth like the Eagle, Throughout these 2 millenia of travail our historic portrait has been painted in blood and fire. Yicheiyainew me yomeiyim urayom hasheleeshee yikee mainu venichyeh lefawnur. He has preserved us throughout the 2 millenia of persecution and frustration. Oovyom hashelleeshee. At the appointed time, on that day we shall prevail. Our existence shall be forever heralded among the nations. Oovawoo goyim leoraw. Nations shall come and admire our spiritual light and our culture glow.

Throughout all our trying times whether there were external problems, pogroms, holocausts or they were internal frustrations we have always envisaged that the candle of G-d shall forever glow. The Rabbis comment that before the sun of Eli set, there arose the sun of Samuel. The rock of Israel shall arise to extricate us from our plight as we have experienced in our own time the rebirth of our nation in its homeland. The third day has come about. The 3rd commonwealth is about to flourish and prosper once again. Tzur Yisroel as we know symbolizes G-d. G-d is depicted as the Rock of Ages, the fortress of our timeless heritage. Let us examine further this concept of Tzur Yisroel, the idea that G-d is a rock, symbol of strength. There is an inner meaning to be explained in the semantics of Tzur. The term Tzur can also mean "binding" being ultimately bound with Almighty G-d. Just as man cannot escape from G-d. "Can man hide in the crevices and I, G-d, shall not see him?" Is there any abode where man can flee from Almighty G-d? Indeed the entire problem of Jonah expresses this very concept that there is no escape from his Almighty Presence, from His Omnipresent character. The only escape is unto Him, being bound and interrelated, cleaving unto Him. However G-d also is inextricably intertwined with man, G-d cannot extricate himself and cease to come to man's aid to deliver him from the ensuring peril from which he is engulfed. Though we are immersed in great torment G-d is also involved in our peril, in our suffering.

In all of man's anguish, G-d is also concerned and He shall rescue him in his time of travail. *Harzoree ain b'Gilud im rofeh ain shun?*

Is there no doctor in Gilead to help him? Tzur is semantically involved in the idea of healing, in the idea of extricating man from the plight of his peril, alleviating him from his ensuing suffering. G-d then as the Rabbis portray, the Eternal Architect, shall attire man ultimately in the original of the First Man, Adam Harishon.

In future times, our Rabbis tell us, G-d shall take the sun out of the enclosed case, the essential light. The righteous shall become healed by it; the wicked shall be devoured. The prophet exclaims in a deep sense of regret, how Israel has proclaimed that G-d has forsaken her.

G-d has forgotten me and has neglected us (Isaiah). Can a woman forget her offspring? And G-d declares: I can never forget! Israel perhaps thought that she is small and insignificant that G-d should take cognizance of her and extricate her from her suffering and exile. However, man has been created *btzelem elokim* in the shadow of Almighty G-d. Just as man cannot be divorced from his shadow, so G-d likewise, cannot and will not divest himself of man when he calls unto Him. Ultimately there will be a Yeshuah, a redemption. On the heels of the Hitler Holocaust and the intensive aggravating tragedy we have also experienced a new dawn, a new era in Jewish history, the rebirth of our nation. The Tzelem Elokim must prevail, for G-d is Nitzchius, everlasting so man must ultimately be redeemed. Tzelem means Tzel shadow and similarly it means hatzolah, salvation and redemption. In the place where Adam was created, our Rabbis tell us that mizbaiach, the altar of Kaporah, of cleansing our iniquities was erected and constructed upon this very terra firma upon which man was created. Therein is his geulah redemption. Therein lies his eternal task to be ultimately tied and inextricably linked with Almighty G-d, with dvaikus bahashem. Adam Harishon is the classic hymbol that although man falls and slips into the abyss of self-destruction and self-corrosion there is a road wherein he can be elevated and uplifted. In our darkest times, in all the ages of despondency, G-d calls to man reminding him that salvation and redemption can be found. When ye shall be filled in anguish and all these troubles shall engulf you—then man will cry from the depths of the sea; From the innermost recesses of his spiritual resources, He calls out and declares that the only way for man is to make the movement of upward spiritual mobility. To begin to climb up the path of finding and exploring His essence. All the external phenomena that we can experience in sensing the world about us and all the internal development of our ideas, cultural growth are to explore the way of G-d that we may approach this idea of continuity. There is a continuity between man and man and this precious continuity is linked up between man and G-d and man and G-d are inextricably bound up—one to the other: Ani l'dodi, v'dodi li.

The task of the prophet is to bring consolation and continued hope to Israel. This self-evident and quite apparent from the vision of the dry bones in which G-d conveys the message of redemptive hope and rejuvenating spirit to the Prophet Ezehiel.

"Shall these dry bones become rejuvenated," ask G-d of Ezehiel and Ezehiel responds, "I don't know," and G-d delivers the answer that they shall be resurrected. The Psalmist, on the other hand expresses his desire of a ceaseless tie between man and G-d, an uninterrupted chain in the cultural aspirations and spiritual designs of mankind. Mipi olilim v'yonkim yeesaditaw oz.

Out of the mouths of babes and sucklings Thou hast established Thy strength. To destroy the enemy and those that seek Thy vengeance. What is man that Thou shalt concern Thyself with him and son of man that Thou should give cognizance to him? The answer is indicative of the idea that there is a certain continuity to mankind. In the advancing stage of humanity there is hope and there is aspiration to cleave unto G-d, to adhere to His concepts, to study His law aspiring to be sanctified like Him. It is noteworthy how Cain constructed a city after he had brutally murdered his brother, Abel. What is the relationship between Cain's prior act of fratricide to his atonement of building a city, of constructing an urban settlement. The idea is that there is continuity to mankind and when Cain slew his brother, he destroyed that continuity, he uprooted, he discontinued the ongoing process of mankind, he stripped humanity of its growth and development. Then He realized the great atrocity that he had committed and he decided to reconstruct society at that particular time. He decided that he must make his contribution to civilization and rebuild it giving further stability to society. The building of great communal centers is a step forward in creating worthwhile cultural centers that will give further growth and greater stimulus to the idea of continuity, of G-dliness. Now Cain we learn stood up against Abel his younger brother and he slew him. There are many ways that people can slay their fellowman. In our society, man commits great atrocities upon his fellow man in a subtle manner —in a passive, omissive way as the prophet decrees. Yawsom lo yishpotoov'riv almanah lo yawvo ahlaihem. They do not judge the orphan and the quarrel of the widow does not come to their counsel.

They are not concerned, involved in the plight and predicament of the unfortunate and handicapped. The plight of the poor is none of their concern. They would rather associate themselves with the rich, with the mighty, Isaiah continues. Koolo chaiv shochad v'rodaif shalmonim.

They all love bribery and they pursue present-taking.

Constructing communal centers is to be pursued in a purely idealistic way without the pursuit of mundane material pleasure. We must rather channel our energies, devote our strength toward building a more responsible society—a community that cares for one another. Hence in the portion of the Torah describing the birth of Noah and all the incidents that led up to the life of Abraham, we read about the great iniquities, the great lust and splendor by the men of that generation, 2 great crimes were committed, 2 great iniquities and 2 great sins, 2 great transgressions, the chayt of the mahbel and dor hafluguh. The generation of the deluge. They are called the generations that were consumed, over come by the flood and the generations who were dispersed by G-d. After man becomes enamoured by the mundone pleasures, becomes enticed by the various seductive elements in society that allure him and ensnare him from the path of righteousness and from the Divine Road of Sanctity he slips from his ultimate image of tzelem Elokim into the dismal abyss of sheol tachtiyaw, of sliding away from the proper goals and aims and motivations that are his spark of G-dliness. Thus the Bible takes account of 2 generations that reflected 2 varied approaches of man's evil outlook and his prideful approach against Almighty G-d. The generation of the Flood is characterized by man's drive after pleasure, the pursuit for lust and anxiety for passion. Our sages declare that the flood, the gzar din, the decree of the Flood was sealed only because of the lust for robbery, conniving and chicanery, man's cheating his friend also engaging in illicit relationships pursuing licentious cohabitation. The dor haflugah the generation who took counsel against G-d, saying "Let us build a tower" committed a different kind of atrocity. It was man's intellectual rebellion against G-d, declaring that he, alone in creative, he alone is productive. It was a denial of G-d's singular creativity that man is omnipotent and man is omniscient. Thus we have a contrast between these 2 generations. One is a material atrocity, a material sin. The other is an intellectual sin against G-d. All throughout society, men in their vain passion and sophisticated cultural approaches have sought to deny and to undermine the Almighty with these 2 methods. In both instances, after man decays, either materially or spiritually, as we have seen in the dor hamahbel and dor haflugah God, as it were, extends His hand to uplift man from his downfall. G-d commanded Noah once again to be fruitful and multiply. Also after the disperson of the Towers of Babel Ninrod became a mighty king of Babylon. Wherein G-d had dispersed man, there he made a center of government for Nimrod. There Nimrod became the first governmental leader. Thus there is continuity in life although man commits and perpetuates great atrocities and great iniquities. Almighty G-d seeks to retrieve man and His desire is to extricate man from the plight of his unreasonabel and inane acts.

Likewise the Jews in the wilderness committed 2 great errors: chait hawaigel and chait ham'roglim
The Sin of the Golden Calf was an expression of man's desire for the pursuit of pleasure of inane material splendour that seeks to ensnare man and allure him from the path of ultimate spirituality. The sin of listening to Moses spies which he dispatched to Canaan was an intellectual one, a denial of Almighty

G-d's universal supervision, in particular, His guidance of the community of Israel. In Judaism there are commandments and concepts that express the duties of the heart and the duties of the limbs, internal duties and external activities. With this Judaism declares that there are 2 methods, 2 approaches to become ultimately committed, cleaving unto G-d. Internal commitment and external adherence are necessary functions for the dynamic process of continuity. We must be alert in our external acts and we must also have the creative capacity of establishing internal vibrant structure that will give vitality to Judaism, to our Jewish living, making our contribution to the world civilization ever greater. V'nahhahroo ailuv kol hagoyim.

All the nations shall flow to the Jewish community, not only flow in numbers nahharoo but also nahharoo as the commentators explain become enlightened.

Before Abraham and Sarah can give birth to Isaac G-d commands Abraham to circumrise himself, to observe the mitzvoh of milah. It is noteworthy that in connection with certain episodes we have an account of the mitzvoh of milah preceding that particular story.

As we noted, before Sarah can conceive of giving birth to Isaac, Abraham was commanded to circumcise his foreskin. Before the Jews enter Israel G-d commands Joshua to take a knife carved out of rock and to circumcise those Jews who were not able to be circumcised in the desert. Also before Moses returned to Egypt to be the messenger of redemption for his brethren, we are told that Zypporah, his wife, took a rock and circumcised her sons. The question arises then, what is the philosophic purpose and theologic significance behind the mitzvoh of circumcision in regard to these particular episodes. The mitzvoh of milah reminds us that, every day, man must dedicate and consecrate himself unto G-d. Abraham was told of birth bain habsorim, the covenant of pieces that were severed when G-d passed between them. There He conveyed to him the message that his children would be a chosen people. What then is this other covenant of circumcision? It is precisely that circumcision reminds us constantly, everyday, that man from his eighth day onward is continually exercising his religious consciousness. The Jew must make a sacrifice unto G-d every day of his life. However, the brith bain habsorim was a sign of singular significance. It was striking and grasping but only momentarily that Abraham was overwhelmed and awestricken by the tardaimah, the slumber that overtook him. This was the miraculous experience of the brith bain habsorim. Milah, then declares to man that he must be dedicated and devoted unto G-d. Thus, too, when G-d says to Joshua: Circumcise the people for thy have not done so in the desert, and then the text continues with this almost unexplainable reason. For today I have revealed and disclosed the abomination of Egypt amidst you. How can the shame of Egypt be removed by exercising the mitzvoh of milah? The Egyptians also believed in G-d for after several of the plagues, Pharoah said G-d is righteous and I and my people are guilty.

What then was the lack of belief that Pharoah displayed against G-d? Pharoah perhaps believed that there was a supernatural being, that G-d would intervene. However He was not eager to admit or anxious to surrender himself with the total commitment to G-d that man assumes with the realization that G-d is omnipotent, omnipresent and omniprevalent. To this Pharoah would not be inclined to agree. Oh yes, he would perhaps agree that G-d could come, flash by, Momentarily he was impressed and overwhelmed by a supernatural G-d. That G-d displays his intervention every day, every moment, in every breath that man inhales and exhales to this Pharoah was not ready yet to surrender himself. Hence for this, Moses had to circumcise his sons before he entered Egypt as a symbol that G-d is with Israel every moment, that man must make a sacrifice not at certain intervals of time but as a steady process, not whimsically as man so desires. This is perhaps the assurance that G-d has expressed with the personality of Abraham, that he will communicate to his children the concepts and ideals to do righteous deeds and noble acts. It is not merely at a striking moment that man can be overwhelmed and overtaken by the idea of G-d. It is through constant dedication and ever alert diligence that man strives to identify himself with G-d and thereby cleaving to his essence.

I am gladdened about thy precepts as one who finds great spoil on the battle fields. The mizvoh of milah to which Rabbis have ascribed this sentence is indicative of the idea that the continuity of life is a ceaseless battle. This mizvoh of milah of being consecrated and dedicated to G-d without any interruption in a permanent and ceaseless manner can prepare man and make him ever ready and ever fit on the battlefield of life, to conquer the enemy of self-deception and self corruption.

Through the constant sacrifice unto G-d that is personified by the precept of circumcision, Abraham's complaint of not having a child to carry on and continue in the way of G-d is resolved by the birth of his son, Isaac. Let us contrast the character of Abraham with that of Noah and we will discern the distinction between the two personalities as they have been recorded in our Bible. We have previously discussed the idea that the concept of circumcision is one of everlasting significance which permeates our soul everyday as a daily process in the Jewish religious experience. The brith ben habsorim is a striking event that overtakes us instantly and makes us experience a feeling of being overwhelmed and excited. This momentary event coupled with the concept of milah which expresses the idea of gradation, are the two covenants which G-d conveyed to Abraham. The Brith ben habsorim represents striking dynamic revelation of G-d, and the mitzvoh of milah expresses the daily process, the almost uneventful, the seemingly inconsequential supervision of Almighty G-d over Israel. This very tzoor that Zipporah took to cut off and sever the orlah, the foreskin, this rock which is termed tzoor and sever the orlah, the foreskin, this rock which is termed tzoor binds the Jew ultimately unto G-d. The tzoor which separates is that instrument which ultimately binds and connects man to his creator. Thus in Joshua, we read take a charvos tzoorim, a rock that cuts.

When they took the tzoor in that age, in that epoch, when they took the rock to sever the everlasting shame of Egypt they severed the binding materialism, the crushing, mundane, superficiality of Materialism, of Egypt. This rock gave man an ultimate mission, an everlasting purpose, a continued commitment to Almighty G-d. Thus we read. V'yeetzer ha shem elokim ess hawadom awfur min hawadamah. G-d formed man out of the dust of earth. The term v'yeetzer is strikingly picturesque for tzoor, the binding, G-d's creation of man binds man unto G-d. There is a v'yeetzer, shnai yeetzorim. Why two yoods this v'yeetzer? Perhaps we can suggest a meaning for the two yoods in the word v'yeetzer, one expresses relationship between G-d and man, the other between man and G-d. Both are inextricably intertwined and G-d will never sever His bond with mankind and mankind will always cleave unto G-d. Man must reach out into something which is beyond his immediate material and mundane existence, something which elevates hi mto a plateau of salvation. There are two classic stories of creation and perhaps these 2 dicta seem to contradict each other. The Rabbis declared that B'asorah m'amoros nivraw hawolum. In 10 declaration the world was created.

Another dictum relates B'hee borum, b'hai borum. This is the story of heaven and earth when they were created with a 'heh'. With the mere utterance, the opening of the mouth, so to speak, they were created. From the B'asorah m'amoros we see gradation, a process of movement, day by day, slowly, step by step, B'hee borum is momentous, it's instantaneous, it's overwhelming, it's magnetic. B'hai borum immediately, striking, dynamic, the 2 creations, the process making of the would. B'asorah m'amoros and the momentous making of the world B'heeborum are 2 sides of 1 issue, as it were. They both complement each other and express the idea that man must declare himself in his ultimate relationship to G-d, in both ways. As we have stated concerning the idea of creation, there are 2 categories wherein man expresses his ultimate relationship G-d, namely the steady process the slow, upward mobility towards G-d and the dynamic, overwhelming, shattering process of one's religious relationship to G-d. Likewise, we see these twofold concepts concerning redemption. There is a geulah that comes in the form of graduation, step by step, slowly, spiralling through the rugged course of the rough road on the ultimate path of redemption. "Sholchainee Kee awlaw hashachar," declared the Angel whom Jacob wrestled, "Send me away for the morning star has arisen."

When a man wrestled and quarreled with our Patriarch

Jacob, it symbolized that there is a long trail of travail that will, at times, overturn, at times overwhelm. It will shatter at times and it will uproot the Jew from settlement to settlement, from place to place.

In 10 places the divination experienced exile and also in 10 exiles the Sanhedrin was displaced and the Jewish Community as well, had its long road of exile. In our times we have experienced redemption. This has come about as a process of Kimaw, Kimaw Kaalos hashachar. Breath by breath, spiralling and almost to the point of expiring, we have experienced a new dawn, new sahchar, a new star of redemption, a rebirth of our nation. Here, however, is also the experience of momentous intervention, of striking salvation that grasps man and does not let him fall. One could contrast the two exiles, namely Babylonia and Rome, in this manner.

The former exile and its following redemption came about miraculously, spectacularly while the latter, the exile of Rome and the return to Judea has been a long drawn out return. This perhaps, to some degree expresses the thought of Ki mairuchok niraw ailei hashem. From a great distance has G-d appeared to me.

One cannot see the presence of the Shechina when he is in such close proximity. He must observe it from a distance and at times, however we experience the Shechina in a relationship of Korov hashem l'chol Korov.

G-d is nigh unto all who call upon him, to all who proclaim his Essence.

This relationship of our National historic heritage was expressed within the personality of Abraham. Indeed, he reflects and mirrors the entire portrait of our people. Abraham expresses his desire to intercede on behalf of Sodom in the manner. V'awnochi awfur vawaifer.

I have but dared, to speak, Almighty G-d, to express my discontent, and to voice my disapproval and yet I am but dust and ashes. On the one hand Abraham appears as tremendous, awesome, magnificent with great splendor, yet he experiences a feeling of nihility, of nothingness, worthlessness as if he were altogether nonexistent. As the psalmist declares.

What is man that thou givest cognizance to him and son of man that thou should consider him. But you have made him little less than G-d and you have adorned him in splendor and magnificence.

Similarly, thy righteousness is up at the mountains, O G-d and thy judgement is at the abyss. Extreme greatness ascending to harai El and an immense feeling of nothingness thom rabaw is singularly coupled and united in one phrase. This is the striking duality that encompasses man and expresses his ever existing dilemma. Man is the synthesis between spirit and flesh, between body and soul. G-d likewise, expresses himself unto man as being at one and the same time, transcendant and imminent, the simultaneous dual relationship. Mee Kadoshem elohainu hamagbeehee lawshawvess hamashpeelee leeros bashomayim uvawawretz.

He is above and far removed from us and also lowers himself to witness and observe what is doing on heaven and earth.

What is the character of Abraham and how does it express itself within the context of intellectual Jewish History and creative Judaism? How do we contrast and compare it with Noah?

The ideas of Universalism and Particularism are not foreign to anyone who is versed in Theology. Noah symbolizes the Universalistic approach, the Universal cognition of G-d and Abraham of course, is the particular expression of experience through Israer, Klal Yisroel. We find Noah building an ark and seeking safety and flight from the flood. G-d tells Noah:

Kaits kol bausur baw efawnei.

The termination of entire mankind has come before me and its destruction is imminent for they have transgressed and sinned greatly, committed many atrocities, G-d then, commands Noah to build an ark according to certain architectural specifications. Then G-d erases the entire civilization at that particular age in history and Noah is spared above all. After the deluge is terminated, the flood has ceased and the soil once again is rejuvenated, G-d tells Noah that he has made a sign that no longer shall flood annihilate mankind. No longer shall people be eradicated by this kind of tempestuous tidal wave. And G-d gave the sign. Ess Kashti nawasathi b'awnun.

My bow I have fixed in a cloud and symbolizing the everlasting covenant of G-d with mankind, that civilization should not be forever terminated.

Let us observe the episode concerning Abraham. Abraham expresses his remorse on behalf of Sodom entreating G-d to save tiny little Sodom from annihilation and destruction. Noah however is completely silent concerning the doomed fatal destruction of the world. Noah does not express any idea, word or notion concerning the eradication and annihilation of all mankind, while Abraham intercedes and pleads for tiny Sodom. The dialogue between G-d and Abraham is moving and appealing. Abraham constantly claiming that there must be some way to preserve sinful Sodom. Abraham then continues incessant plea to G-d. Why is there this striking distinction between Abraham and Noah? What does the Bible mean to convey to us in this lesson? Abraham is the vigilant champion of the principle of social responsibility and personal confrontation for the individual and the group. His grief over the capture of Lot his nephew is coupled with his anguish over the deterioration and disintegration of Sodom. Abraham is overpowered and awestricken by a sense of ultimate responsibility and everlasting commitment to the supreme ideal that we have to be ever diligent and always aware of our fellow man. The Rabbis keenly observe an inherent distinction between Abraham and Noah.

With regard to Noah we find ess Elohim hishalaich Noah. Noah walked with G-d. In regard to Abraham we read Hishalaich l'fawnei veheyai tomim. Walk before me, carry the trail, be a trailblazer, be a pathfinder. This is the character of Abraham, go before me, precede, dynamism, while Noah only walks with G-d. Noah is passive, Abraham is active. Va yorawtz. Abraham ran to be machnis orchim. Abraham, alone, the man who had extreme wealth and abundance of economic security couldn't he not tell his servants to secure the well-being of the 3 angels who came to visit him. No, Abraham himself had to intercede, he had to demonstrate his feeling for his fellowman towards the angels. Abraham, asks G-d for a sign, a significant symbol wherein there shall be continuity. G-d tells him he shall have continuity. While Noah who was completely passive to the idea of continuity, had to be told that there would be continuity. Abraham demands continuity. Noah is only agreeable to continuity. Herein lies the distinction between Abraham and Noah.

After Abraham has experienced responsibility and assumed nis obligation towards the 3 angels, toward Lot and towards Sodom, we get insight into his profound character. However, the final test is yet to come. The classic Akedah where Abraham is commanded to bring up his only son, Isaac, as a sacrifice will he (Abraham) remain true to the challenge? Will he demonstrate the steadfastness of his character and the perseverance of his personality? Abraham has already been frustrated about Ishmael when Sarah was caught up in conflict with her maiden, Harar, and was forced to set Hagar and Ishmael free. Abraham was perplexed for he had no longer Ishmael at his side and now he was to be set apart from Isaac divorced completely from continuity, distraught and despondent. He set upon his new nesoyan (his challenge and test) with vigor and energy to meet the tiresome trial of the Akedah-of binding his son Isaac for sacrifice of whom G-d said, with Isaac shall your descendants be considered.

This dream was for Abraham, being swept away from reality cast aside and, abraham had now to face the darkness and disillusion and despair of being severed from Isaac, cut asunder from continuity and separated from the ongoing process of his tradition, his ideology.

Now we imagine that the Akedah was a crucial test for him to control his temper and contain his emotion. There are many problems in the saga of the Akedah. One, what is the uniqueness, the challenge of the Akedah for in all religions, men have brought human sacrifice of their first born. Secondly, why did Abraham tell his servants:

You remain with the donkeys and Isaac and I will go to the altar. Why could Abraham not bring his servants with him? Then, towards the end of the classic event, G-d tells Abraham "Now I know that you are the true servant of G-d, that you rever G-d." Was not G-d knowledgeable of this fact prior to the Akedah? After Abraham had displayed his immense concern for Lot and Sodom, this test, this challenge, plays a special role in discerning the true character and nobility of Abraham. We could have imagined that Abraham's zeal and zest for his concern and compassion toward Lot and Sodom was a result to enhance and advance his own self-glorification and self-aggrandizement. It perhaps, could have represented Abraham's desire to succeed only because he wanted to find grace in the eyes of his peers, in the eyes of the people about him. These noble acts alone could not evidence a true religious figure. Perhaps Abraham had ulterior goals and material motives to express and achieve. Therefore, the test of the Akedah represents a true vindication of Abraham's noble soul. G-d told him to bring Isaac as a spiritual sacrifice unto him. Could Abraham stand this test? Could he stand alone against such insuperable odds, insurmountable problems that he would no longer envisage continuity? Abraham who had attained such splendor, who had experienced such grandeur and glory in the eyes of his kinsmen, in the eyes of humanity, could he withstand the pressure and overcome the obstacle of standing alone and losing everything that he had amassed. Losing, being lost being a failure, experiencing failure, could Abraham be a servant of G-d in this manner? Therefore, Abraham tells his servants, shevoo l5chem. Stand alongside the caravan and Isaac and I shall walk alone to our rendezcous, in our spiritual mission, in our moment of true trial. Abraham is ready to assume all failure marking the true example of the great spiritual figure of Abraham. Ohtaw Yawdahti kee Yorai elohim ataw.

Now I know, now it has been proven that, it has been demonstrated that you, Abraham, are the true reverer of Almighty G-d. For you have wagered to sacrifice your son in time of trial. You have everything to lose and nothing to gain. Still you have been willing to accept whatever is to be.

After the Akedah story we see a remarkable contrast between Abraham and Noah and Lot.

When Noah and Lot were vindicated and redeemed from stress and sorrow, they immediately became sheKurim, sluggards, drank wine and committed sinful acts—acts of transgression against G-d. For drinking, itself, is a Meedaw sheainaw hagunaw atrocious and immoral act. After Noah and Lot were vindicated they then slid to the abyss of spiritual decay. Noah cursed Ham who uncovered and disclosed the shame of his father. Lot committed incest with his two daughters. However, Abraham is quite apart and distinguished from these 2 figures. His religiosity is complete, his idealism has been fulfilled to the utmost. He has ascended to the ultimate pinnacle of his spiritual aim, unto Almight G-d. He now commands his servant Eliezer to find a suitable spouse for his son Isaac. He does not slumber and become a sluggard. He does not slip and slide from the path of spiritual progress. Abraham remains on this high plateau and intends to climb yet higher. Abraham is also concerned for his wife, Sarah. V'yawvo Abrohom lispaid es Soroh v'livkowaw.

After Sarah passed away, Abraham expresses his grief, anguish and sorrow over the departure of his beloved wife. He does not want to acquire the m'oros hamachpailaw as a gift from Efron. Rather he intends this to be something of a concrete expression of his love for Sarah. He is not getting a present. He aims to display his true friendship for Sarah. His real concern is evident. Not to obtain a gift for her trying merely to fulfill his obligations, rather he wants to fulfill his responsibility with nobility. Isaac too desires to emulate his father. Vayaitzai yitzoch lawsooach ha sawdeh.

Isaac went out in the field to pray, to meditate. Will Rivkah follow in the footsteps of his mother, Sarah? Will she be able to carry on, to continue the home life that his parents were able to maintain? Will Isaac be able to uphold the cultural gains that his parents have advanced? Isaac was satisfied that Rivkah is able to continue in the path of Sarah for Rivkah said to Eliezer, drink and also for your camels I shall give water. Rivkah has a concern not only for human life but for the entire species of life. Rivkah displays and exhibits the true social universal concern for all living things. This is the example that the patriarchs symbolize in expressing, advancing and enhancing the concept, ideology and principles of the ethics of G-d.

Kee yidahtee—I know that his (Abraham's descendants will fulfill admirably the tradition to do righteous acts and noble deeds for all times. Abraham we have previously contrasted with Noah. However there is one definite similar parallelism that is strikingly significant and closely interwoven with one another. Abraham and Noah both entered into a threefold relationship with G-d, covenant, oath and grace. Covenant is a mutual relationship. Oath is one wherein G-d binds himself unto man and swears that there will be continuity for everlasting time. Grace is the relationship wherein man who does not deserve any lasting kindness from G-d because of his inevitable manner of disgracing himself before Him and who is considered to be breyaw shefailaw being filled with desire for passion and amassing great material splendor and economic gain is nevertheless graced by G-d for eternity. Now the Brith, Chesed, Shevooah relationship is identical both to Abraham and Noah. Abraham and Noah have both been ultimately bound up with G-d on this tripartite level. The world community, the universal community and Jewish community, the particular community have parallel and intersecting lines. They are equal and apart. They have common functions and also the Jewish community has its own destiny, its own historic heritage to perform. Abraham tells Ephron the Hittite Ger V'toshuv anochi besochem, I am a stranger and a sojourner and also a citizen. Abraham realizes at once his dual relationship. He is both a transient settler and a permanent citizen. He has his own destiny to perform however not disassociating himself from the general community at large. Abraham is quick to tell the King of Sodom that Awne eshkol and mamreh. They shall share in the material wealth with you. However, I have my own role, my own goals, my own challenges and my own expectations. Isaac also, hen he tells Jacob, "The voice is the voice of Jacob and the hands of Esau" has also tried to communicate to Jacob that he must reconcile his personal and particularized identity, his own separate and communal and religious, cultural and spiritual commitments to observe. However, he must also be abreast of the generalized other community—to reconcile these two is the task of Jacob. V'Yaacob eesh tam yoshaiv oholeem dwelling in both tents, understanding his own heritage, his own destiny and simultaneously being knowledgeable of the general total other community is Jacob's role. This is precisely what the angel declares to Jacob-Kee sawreesaw im elohim vim ahnoshim v'tuchol. "You have been challenged and confronted by both man and G-d and you have conquered. You have spiralled up to a sublime, religious summit; your goals have reached the heaven while standing firm and steadfast on the ground. The dream of sulom mutzov artsaw v'rosho mageeah hashomanimaw has been realized. Jacob's ideal has been fully exemplified. Although his cultural expectations are mageeah, ascending to the limitless boundaries, nevertheless, his feet, his physical and social needs are mootzuv artzah, they are with the community-at-large, the entire communiy. The Rabbis drew the inference from the phrase in Isaiah—"House of Jacob, go and proceed in the light of G-d." Unlike Abraham who called unto G-d at the mountain, not like Isaac who called unto G-d on the field. And Yitzoch went out into the field to have his confrontation with G-d. Rather Jacob called unto G-d in the "house" bayis-to demonstrate the idea of G-d's sovereignty with material matters. Not to set aside, to isolate and to segregate oneself from the mundane, material matters that persist at every step of one's life, not to alienate oneself from the world community, rather, Jacob was to sublimate and transform the material into higher and more fruitful spiritual goals. This is the declaration of Jacob, Kee soreesaw, challenging the world, confronting civilization at all levels, two camps, machnayim that Jacob refers to are the camp of the general community, of understanding the world on the universal level and the camp of the personalized, private community. When Jacob finally confronted his father-in-law Laban they made a pact which Laban called yeegar sahadoosaw and Jacob called gal aid. Jacob retains his own spiritual aspirations in terming the altar that they had erected in Hebraic language while Laban used his native Aramaic tongue. We may infer from this that Jacob, although able to make a pact with Laban, clung to his own culture and continued in the ways of his fathers. When also Joseph came to Jacob later after the long travail that Joseph had incurred, had experienced, we find him asking his father to bless Menashe and Ephraim. Consequently, Jacob blesses Ephraim with his right hand and Menashe with the left. Joseph wanted to intercede that Menashe should get the blessing with the right because he was the elder. Menashe should be blessed with a greater blessing. No, Jacob intervenes and blesses Ephraim because Ephraim symbolizes the ideal of being fruitful, of being productive in the confrontation with other cultures. Menashe symbolizes assimilation with the other cultures, abandoning his own personal identity with Jewish culture, ideology, heritage. Now the problem—why can Jacob easily conceive with Leah while experiencing difficulty in conceiving with Rachel. Leah symbolizes the idea of lawoh, conflict, challenge and confrontation—to overcome the problem obstacles and pitfalls that are prevalent in one's everyday life. Leah was able to accept, adjust and understand her particular culture and not to assimilate, abandon her own culture. Rachel, on the other hand, symbolizes the idea of rach, soft, smooth, fine, pleasant. This connotes a kind of passivity-being passive and apathetic in the face of conflict and challenge. However, when Rachel complains to Jacob and Jacob says, "Am I in place of G-d"? Now Jacob understood and asserted himself and was able to overcome and override the obstacles and perils that make one complacent and self-righteous. He was no longer apathetic, passive. Rather he was made alert and aware of the problems that arise. And he can and will persever in the environment of Rachel which symbolizes pleasure and splendor. We can understand why in parsha v'yaishev as soon as it says, "This is the history of Jacob," "this is the genealogy of Jacob," there is an abrupt entering into the history of Joseph. Because Joseph symbolizes productivity and fruitfulness in the light of challenge the entire history and drama that is portrayed in his character in one that expresses and champions his culture and civilization. Yoseph hoo hamazhbeer l'chol ambawawretz. Joseph is the one who communicates and transmits the ideas and ideals of his par excellence, the concept understanding his own personalized, private and particular culture while simultaneously being aware and cognizant of the generalized universal, other community.

Let us now reflect on the character of Jacob—how it is depicted in the Bible and how he is described as the Patriarch who personified truth. Teetain emmess l'yaacov.

Previously we have portrayed the exemplary and noble

chesed of Abraham. Now we present the truth, the emmes of Jacob. If one can harmonize these two attributes of chesed and emmes, one can aspire to the exemplary religious figure. We are quite familiar with the episode concerning Jacob and Esau, Jacob wrested the Torah and likewise, the B'chowaw from his brother, Esau. This dual complaint that Esau had against his younger brother, Jacob, is expressed in his deceit and hatred, trying to perpetuate and contrive fratricide against his brother Jacob. Henceforth, Jacob flees, seeks refuge at his Mother's family—Laban—in Padan Aram. The problem is did Jacob really deceive Esau and if so, why was Jacob consequently deceived by his father-in-law, Laban, when Jacob took Leah instead of Rachel. Jacob remained several years after to marry Rachel. Why was Jacob who if we assume was a conniving personality, why didn't he assert his shrewdness and why was he led into deception by his father-in-law Laban. Esau blames Jacob for being fooled. Is this really so? When we read that Esau and Jacob decided to trade the B'choraw Esau does not admit this fact to his father Yitzchok. Rather he conceals it from him. Esau is not willing to disclose the fact to his father that he had sold his birthright to Jacob. Esaw, on the other hand, seeks again the B'choraw, realizing that with the B'choraw he had lost the blessing. We may infer a dialogue between Esau and Jacob with regard to the B'choraw Esay says, "I am about to die. Why do I need the B'choraw? Why do I need to assume the responsibility and problem of B'choraw, of leading a life of purpose, meaning, direction and goals? I am a hunter seeking prey, wild life and human beings. I am a military man, a man who is a warrior not a dweller in tents, not one who wastes his time in abstract, unimportant phenomena: No, I am concerned with the practical life. Jacob when he bought the B'choraw knew what his responsibility was—that he was accepting a new role, new goals, new dimension and purpose in life. That is why the result of B'choraw is concluded in Brochaw. They are inextricably intertwined and receiving the blessing from his father is a concommitant of assuming social responsibility. Now, too with regard to Laban deceiving Jacob, we find that Jacob does not say, "I'll kill my father-in-law because he has contrived to deceive me." The lesson of the story is in picturesque contrast to that of Jacob and Esau. Esau seeks to keep his vengeance and cast his fury upon his brother Jacob because Jacob had supposedly deceived him. Esau cannot submit to the idea that he, the mighty one, has fallen because of the idea of the abstract concept of Brochaw. Esau has lost out because he has failed to assume his responsibilities and therefore he seeks the blood of his brother, Jacob. Jacob although deceived by his father-in-law does not submit to hateful passion like his bloodthirsty brother. Jacob is willing to assume a submissive quality not to confront Laban in battle as a warrior but rather to wait until the time has come. Ad ya'avor sa'am till the anger or fury passes over, to be patient and to endure.

Until that time comes, long travail has Jacob too experienced. Until the great hour comes, he must go through a horrendous period of holocaust, shattering ages of suffering—until the blissful moment will arrive, until the achriss hoyomim and the redemption will be realized. There is a long period of frustration that is to be overcome—obstacles and perils to be weathered. The contrast of Jacob to Esau is clear. Esau quenches his bloodthirst while Jacob is patient and enduring.

When Jacob however comes to grips with Esau, his brother, they reconcile their differences and Jacob and Esau part on friendly terms. Jacob encounters an angel who wrestled with him the entire night till daybreak. Then the angel was beaten back by Jacob. However, the angel injured him slightly. He requests the angel to bless him and the angel tells him that his name shall no longer be called Jacob—only Israel, because you have confronted G-d and man and you have demonstrated your valiant courage and creative cultural capacity.

The question is apparent, why did Jacob request the Angel's blessing? He had already been blessed by G-d in the previous portion, G-d telling him that he will be prosperous and he will advance to become a mighty nation. He also had his father's blessing.

Why now is there a need for the blessing from the Angel? What is new and what is original within the context of this blessing? Jacob was blessed intimately by his father Yitzchek and G-d confirmed it eternally. The angel, however, is an external universal force beyond Jacob's immediate social milieu. The angel represents the entire world civilization, acknowledging the greatness and intellectual character of the people of Israer. Kee soreesaw em elohim v'eem ahnawsheem vatoochol.

For Jacob is able to reconcile his personal environment with the general environment. That has been not only acknowledged by G-d but from the external world about him.

The problem of Joseph and his brethren is one that always has been a difficult one to resolve. What is the significance behind the entire episode of Joseph with his brethren? After Jacob has resolved to dwell in complacency, the sages remark, "Then began the entire episode of Joseph and his brothers. Joseph was given by his father a Keesohnes passim—a multi-colored, multi-dimensioned garment that he would be able to reconcile his own Jewish identity with the world identity, a many-colored cloak to give light and luster to all his observers evoking their admiration.

Everyone peered and stared at Joseph's external beauty. However, Joseph was the one who recognized his brethren alto' they were not able to recognize him. For Joseph was not only externally but also internally of the patriarchal dynasty. We find, therefore, that when there is external complacency, when the environment about the Jewish nation is secured, then internal problems arise, internal frustrations appear. Aileh toldos yaacov—

This is the history and the genealogy of Jacob. Almost abruptly we swing over to Joseph, skipping all his other brethren. Then we come to the long, perilous and arduous episode concerning Joseph being sold into slavery and finally arising as the master of all Egypt. His influence has also been exerted throughout the entire Egyptian civilization. The brethren were not able to compromise, to conciliate their idea of Judaism with the world about them. This has been evidenced, proven and demonstrated in the episode of Shechem Shimon and Levi were the generals who annihilated Shechem because of his illicit relations with Deenah. The other brothers were different from Joseph. They could not wrestle with the total problems of the general civilization about them. Now in the story of Joseph, we find he was cast into slavery caused by his brethren soon after this he was cast into prison. Then as soon as Joseph hit the last rung on the ladder of descent he begins to rise and spiral up the spiritual ladder, ascending to the summit of his personal fulfillment when the portrayal of the story appears at its gloomiest point. Then the supernatural miraculous intervention occurs. A climb that will conclude with the ultimate leadership and mastery of all Egypt. The drama unfolds and the scene on the arena is presented as an exemplary reflection of our entire Jewish history. The Jewish heritage has never failed even in its most dismal hour. Netzach Yisroel loh yeeshawker, proclaims Samuel. The everlasting and timeless quality of the Jewish people shall always prevail throughout the entire travail of its historic march and its cultural development. In the Joseph narration we find a curious incident that Judah married a foreign woman a Canaanite who bore him children but they died. Then he was confronted seductively by Tamar who had disguised herself. She convinced him that he was the one who supposedly had committed adultery. The commentators explain the idea that Judah was compelled to carry out the mitzvah of Levirate. Therefore she was able to live with him. However, there is something significant that within the context of Joseph we find Judah first marrying a Canaanite woman, Tamar committing an illegitimate act, to which he had to submit and then agreeing to the fact that she was righteous—more than he. What is the moral lesson that we have to deduce from this interluding incident? Why was it interjected in the story of Joseph? This lesson exposes one to great morality and high ethical virtue. If we begin to slip and backslide into the pitfalls of committing atrocities and we perpetuate acts of violence, we are apathetic to injustice that is being committed. Then we shall transgress and commit other sins. Wherein a steadfast and courageous moral standard had been maintained, now society begins to slide back and degenerate becoming devoid of human feeling. This is what happened to Judah because he was supposed to react to the unjust perpetration against Joseph and he was silent. He told his father, "This is the blood of Joseph and thus Judah was embarrassed and put to shame by Tamar because he was not earnest and he was not outspoken against the atrocities and transgressions that were committed against Joseph by his brethren. So he was to be exposed and disgraced. Likewise Eeyov needon beshteekaw.

The Rabbis comment: Why was Job exposed to so much suffering, so much hardship? Because he should have expressed his discontent and his feelings of contempt to Pharoah who had taken counsel of him about the Jewish problem. One cannot keep silent when it is time to talk—to decry the evils of society. We cannot disengage ourselves, from the atrocities and wrongdoings that are going on. When the brothers reconciled their differences with Joseph, they acknowledged his greatness, his superior character. Avawl ahshaimim ahnachnoo—but we are guilty; we have to assume the burden of guilt for the hardship that we have caused you. Then Joseph asserted himself and declared that it was but the will of G-d that they should be brought together. In Genesis we find see-sawing battles and peacemaking, confrontation and resolution, disharmony and discordancy culminating however, into harmony and unity. We find Lot and Abraham first separating. Abraham tells Lot. Let us separate, let's sever our relationship because it will only result in disagreement and ill-will. Then we find Abraham saving Lot from the ensuing peril of the Kings who fought with Sodom, Isaac and Ishmail at first separated. Ishmail leaving for the midbar, for the wild life in the desert, comes back and reunites with Isaac participating in mourning and sharing in the grief over their bather Abraham. Likewise, Jacob and Esau who at first had great differences and a feeling of malice between them, finally also came to agreement and compromise. Similarly, Joseph with his brethren, where at first there was distrust, hatred, jealousy and anxiety between them, concludes in a harmonious brotherly relationship. So Genesis is the basic foundation of social behavior. Thesis and antithesis moving into new synthesis. Harmony and discord, and then reconciliation and coexistence. The preamble of the Jewish nation wherein the Jewish People shall realize their destiny and perform the mission that they have been delegated to carry out.

EXODUS

Chapter 2

How Israel, the particular society, lived a vibrant and dynamic, useful and fruitful life within the general total community so depicted is Exodus. Moses is the champion vindicator of the Jews in times of trial, in age of stress, in period of torment. He is delegated with the mission and charged with the challenge to extricate the Jews from the plight of their frustration, from the perils of bondage, and from the misery of slavery. And G-d appears to Moses from the burning bush, from the intense lava that bursts forth from the volcano of life, from the torment of struggle; from the torment of struggle, from the turmoil of strife is born the Prophet Moses, the man who is sent by G-d to come to Pharaoh, and is to be appointed with the unique historical task of being the diplomat for Israel. The man who will be considered the singular prophet, lchain avdee Moshe—in my entire house, so to speak, declares Almighty G-d, Moses is faithful, true and trustworthy. This is the man of whom we will speak lo Kum byisroel k moshe ocl. No one in Israel will arise with that vision, with that scope, with that dynamism as Moses. So, this Moses must come to Pharaoh, and G-d declares unto Moses. Raimsateechaw Elohim ifare "I have given you the quality of being a master to Pharaoh. When you'll come to Pharaoh, you'll not come asking for charitable acts. You'll come with a mission to perform, with goals to achieve and aims to fulfill, as it is written later Vyeekach Moshe maiatzmos Yosef. Moses took from the bones of Joseph, or to paraphrase it, Moses took from the atzmeeyoos from the essence of Joseph, ust as he—the Bible speaks of Joseph as Vchee hoo moshel bchol mitzraim—made his contribution, he performed for the entire total community. Similarly, Moses performed admirably in fulfilling the task of expressing and communicating the mission of G-d and the idea of His Holiness throughout the entire world civilization. This is Moses.

Now, why does Moses marry a daughter of Jethro who was perhaps considered to be outside of the Jewish clan? And Aaron, Moses' brother on the other hand married a daughter of the nobility, Elisheva, bas Aminadav, the daughter of Aminadov, achos Nachshon, the sister of Nachshon, an illustrious family of the aristocracy. Moses married outside of the Jewish nobility. For Moses is alone unique as he is, lo chain avdai Moshe. The mission of Moses is to go and to proselytize, to communicate, and to convey the message of G-d beyond the borders of his own community, outside and above the scope of the limited environment. Moses streaks above the horizon and climbs across the mountainous regions, where no one can climb. He is the Everest of humanity. Wherein the poles of the world dimension come together, as though in a magnetic field and spring forth within his character. Moses, at first is filled with humility, with an overflowing measure of this virtue. He tries to escape this mission, he contends, and moreover the Jews themselves will think so. And Moses is reluctant, and G-d, as it were, is angered over the fact of Moses' inability to extricate himself from the path of apathy. G-d grasped Moses and he caught hold of him, when Moses declared, Asoorana vere es hamare hagodol haze, let me turn away from my pastoral and apathetic life, and see this great sight, this tremendous episode which was going on, a burning bush is on fire and it is not consumed. And G-d appeared to Moses out of the flame of the bush. The call of history is conveyed to Moses. He is delegated with the trying task to extricate the Jews from bondage, to deliver them from slavery, and to set them free on a task and historic mission that will take them on various voyages throughout the millenia, that will ultimately lead to the Messianic era of the prophecies in Isaiah and Micah concerning achris hayomim, the end of time. This is the ideal of

Moses, that he is singular, unique as a prophet, and above many, above all as the leader sine qua non who will convey the continuity of the Jewish historical message, of the Jewish historical dream and of its ideology. That we are an everlasting timeless people, that we'll transcend time, the mundane material world, and the pitfalls, ensnarements, and entanglements that are thrust upon us by the world nations shall be overcome and we shall prevail. No nation can interrupt, can discontinue or put an end to this mission, to this triumphant march in liberating the peoples of the world from the bondage of material conformity, from the slavery of Madison Avenue society. Mizraims Egypt is semantically identified with boundaries, Mazar—with limitations, quantification, and Israel is above and reaches out up over the limting spheres of inffuence, these asphyxiating marks of material controls.

Now, why is Moses delegated with this onerous task, with this supreme mission of delivering the Jews to safety out of the bondage of Egypt? What is so unique in his character, that he is called to the elite mission of restoring Israel to its original glory? Why was Moses delegated for this arduous task and delicate role in extricating Israel from the plight of slavery, from the misfortune of material subjection, from the disastrous situation of oppression? Moses observes G-d and experiences the phenomenon of ultimate commitment unto his Creator from the scene of the burning bush. That Israel, though immersed in a ceaseless stream of suffering, engulfed in a stream of never ending torment indeed shall prevail and it shall arrive, no matter how long it takes to attain its supreme mission of fulfilling its unique historic destiny of communicating and contributing to the world civilization the ideal of the Holy Ethic of Monotheism-Kee am kodosh ataw lailohechaw—that you are a sanctified nation unto Almighty G-d.

Moses sees how an Egyptian lashes his brother Jew, and Moses cannot bear it, he is offended by this. And he smote the Egyptian. Moses, who grew up in the princely home of Pharaoh realizes his concern for his people and at once is overwhelmed with a stream of passion that gushes forth and rushes on to strike out at the Mizri, at the Egyptian. We see Moses also as arbitrating justice between the brethren—one man stood up and attempted to strike his fellow Jew, and Moses, with a sense of responsibility, and a feeling of concern, and an honorable sense of commitment and passion cries out, "Evil man why do you strike your brother?" Moses cannot be apathetic to maltreatment of his brethren and even of one Israelite to another. His character is charged with emotion, raised with that sense of austere responsibility and overwhelming concern that he must take up the cause of justice, assume the noble mission of championing justice. And then we find another episode in the life of Moses, wherein he saved the herd, the flock, of Jethro. Later, thereafter he became the son-in-law of Jethro, as we know. Moses, therefore, not only had a compassion for mankind, he also had a deep emotional feeling towards all the universe, toward animal life as well. Therefore, Moses who is devoted and dedicated toward extricating the Jews from the plight of their suffering, toward liberating them from the yoke of bondage and severing the cord of material and cultural subjection is the one who is designated for delivering Israel. Moses is the one who is infused with the idea and enamored with the concept of continuity for Israel, that there is hatzalah, there is salvation, redemption, and continuity for Israel. Its historic destiny is not an idea for the moment, it is not a precept for one fleeting moment in history. It is rathar, the endless dream of historical identity and ultimate concern with Almighty G-d.

Moses, therefore, is delegated with the call of extricating his people from the plight of bondage and redeeming them from the suffering peril of slavery, because he is a man that is concerned with the peril of his fellow man. We see it in the episode of the Egyptian who attempted to smite the Jew, we see it in te one Jew fighting with his fellow, with his brother, we see it with the animals, with the herd of Jethro, that Moses interceded to save the herd. Hence responsibility and concern is the primal principle upon which there can be predicated the sine qua non, ultimate concept of continuity. And Moses cast asunder the stones of the loochos habrith the tablets of the Ten Commandments only after he had come down from the mountain. He split the stone afterward. The problem raised by the commentaries is why did not Moses break the tablets immediately as G-d told him laich raid—turn away from me because this people has committed atrocity, they are a people of transgressors. Why did Moses wait until he was amidst the crowd, amongst the people? Because Moses the leader is part of the people, he's an integral part of the community, not above or beyond, rather he is within. He is involved in the plight and sorrow and the suffering of his people. When they commit the crime it is as though he would commit the iniquity, when they commit the transgression, it is as though he has gone against the word of G-d. Therefore, he broke the loochos only when he had been amidst the people, that is the true sign of the leader. This, also is why Almighty G-d declared to his people, Kee ani hashem hashochaim eetom besoch toomasom—Within your contaminations, within your defilements, within your abominations, I, Almighty G-d dwell among you, I Almighty G-d live within you, though you have desecrated My Name, defiled My Glory, and defiled My Holiness. Nevertheless, I can I will remain steadfast unto you. G-d has a responsibility and a concern for mankind that there shall never be a severance between Almighty G-d and Klall Yisroel. Even though you are a El Mistater, a G-d who conceals His Glory and the destiny of Israer is shrouded in gloom throughout the millenia of medieval misery and up until 1948, we have envisaged pogrom upon pogrom, calamity upon calamity, and catastrophe upon catastrophe, nevertheless the continuity of Israel has proceeded for its historic, timeless message, because G-d has a responsibility and concern for b chol tzoroaum lo tzur.

That Almighty G-d is bound up with the anguish and agony, with the torment and turmoil, with the frustration, and fear, with all the aggravations and stormy strife that Israel encounters, that Judah encompasses, ha Zion experiences, Almighty G-d is within us. He will never abandon us—bregah Katan azal vitch ubrachamim g'dolim akabsaich—declared the prophet for one fleeting moment have I forsaken, you, however, with great compassion shall I deliver you. Yes tonight is dark and dismal and the dawn of salvation has not yet completely arrived, however we have seen the new birth of Israel, a new redemptive quality for Zion, a new salvation for Judah, that we shall be able to continue as the source of a cultural climate of opinion for all the nations of the world Kee Mitzion tatze Torah for everyone—Kee baisee bais tfilah yekorailchol haamim—thus we see that Torah and worship, the law and the emotion of G-d shall convey its message to the total community, for the entire world civilization at large.

There are two calves or cows that we have been commanded to bring, one is the eglah aroofah and the other is the purah adamah. The eglah aroofah as we have been told in Deuternonomy is brought because a corpse is found in the field and no one knows who slew him. So the Elders of Israel are requested to make the necessary measurement to find the closest city wherein this corpse may have come from and the Elders of that city bring a Korban, a sacrifice unto G-d and they declare, Yawdainoo lo shofcheo hadum hazeh—Our hands have not spilled this blood and our eyes have not seen this atrocity that has occurred. Redeem Thy people and let not clean blood flow in vain. The Rabbis query, can you for a moment think that the elders of Zion, the elders of the city shall have committed such an atrocity as slaying a man? Can you imagine that statesmen, men of high stature, noblemen, scholarly men could commit a violent brutal act—elah—concludes the passage that we have seen him and we have not taken care of his needs, we have not provided for his sustenance, we have not been concerned for his social, economic, and spiritual well-being. This is tantamount to murder, this means committing a crime. Therefore the Elders must proclaim their responsibility for this individual. The poroh adamah symbolizes the responsibility and concern for the total community, that the entire community is responsible, not only for an individual, but for the entire mission and historic heritage of Klal Yisroel. As one unit we are responsible, for the world, for ourselves. The red heifer and the slain calf—asher lo awlaw awlehaw ol—No yoke has come upon it and it has never worked. It has never been taken out to the field. It is completely without any blemish, it's beautiful. The red heifer and the slain calf symbolize the idea that man has completely neglected concern for the fellow man of his community, or for the total community at large. He himself may be pure, beautiful, inwardly and outwardly pious, however he has no concern for others. He has never seen the problems, plight and perils of his brethren, He has never been confronted with the conflicts of his fellowman. Therefore that calf must be burned to ashes to purify and extricate man from the mundane material world that has been set upon us to a sublime spiritual life. No one has concerned himself with that individual who was found slain in the midst of the field. Alone he perished. No one was concerned, no one had compassion, and no one cared. The Torah however cares. Amidst a burning bush when all hope has been given up, when despair has overtaken us, when despondency has overwhelmed us, G-d declares his everlasting bond with Israel, G-d is ultimately bound with Israel. He will never sever his mission lichvodes brawsiv yitzartiv af assesiv—for My honor have I crested thee, formed thee, and shaped thee. Therefore Moses can justly declare Kee hee chochmaschem covesnascham—this is your wisdom and know-how in the eyes of the nations. All our law is predicated on the concept of continuity, that there is an everlasting timeless quality to our historic heritage in our unique masoretic charismatic community which is ultimately bound with the message G-d.

Vhawyawlos al yowdechaw uzikoron bain ainechaw—And this exodus shall be as a symbol on your hand and a sign and a remembrance on your head. The tfilin of the hand and rosh head symbolize a twofold relationship with the world civilization. Namely, reconciling and relating our private and our personal sign with the external and outward sign that everyone should see. Because tfilin sheberosh inferred from th sentence vro rol kee shem ha shem nikraw awlechaw—All the peoples of the world shall see that G-d is inscribed upon you, and they shall revere your. Now the sign on the hand is private, personal, the sign for the head is public. Thus the tfilin of hand and head are a harmony, infusing between the private particular sign and the public, collective or generalized sign. How do we convey this message, and how do we confirm this mission to communicate to the world civilization our heritage and simultaneously not relinquishing our own goals? How do we bridge the gap, and how do we build a relationship that can preserve our identity and convey it, communicate it to the ongoing world civilization? This is related in the Vheegadi taw lvinchaw and vhawyaw kee yisholchaw binchaw. It is by telling your sons and making history a known fact knowledgeable to your children, understandable to the generations, and something that is educational and motivational that will direct them and present them with the proper guidance that they may inspire others and continue the timeless historic heritage. Also, they have to ask questions, ponder. It is not merely enough to tell hem, to present it on a silver platter, to spoon feed them is not the proper attitude. They must be involved and preoccupied with proper questions. We must expose them to the dark side of the moon, so to speak, that they must query, question, and B'machshakim hoshee voonee kmaisaiolam—it's not only that they must see the light always, the great light that's pure and simple. Nothing is always pure and simple. It's a long, rough, rugged road and only through the dense darkness, trotting through the forest of the seemingly forbidding and forboding paths of understanding the Torah, can we understand the principles of life that the Torah has prescribed for us. Navigating the intrepid sea in the Talmud is not an easy voyage to say the least. The journey is arduous, the road is rugged and to reach this plateau at times seems an insurmountable task. Nevertheless, painstaking persistence, perseverance and patience shall make us endure and give us the courage to prevail. Now this twofold cognizance of conveying to our youth, inspiring them with premises and principles, with axioms and theorems is one system. Then, the result of this is that they ask questions and in turn they create, develop principles, theorems, axioms, concepts. By this method we can motivate and inspire, direct and expose the adult youth to understand their culture and continue within the broader cultural milieu of the secular world.

Thus, the exodus from Egypt is accomplished and Israel declares in a clarion voice their pronounced Shirah, homage to G-d, the song of the exodus. Inherent in this poetic passage, is the conquest of nature in serving G-d and the sublime religious activity of transforming and transcending nature in reaching the summit of religious worship. The waters of the sea turned as a wall against Egypt and Bruach a pechaw nermoo mayim—the waters of nature and power of nature became the servants of G-d. Hashem mawluch gayoos lawvaish—G-d has attired himself in a mighty cloak—Afteekon taivel—the entire world is established upon His word, upon His utterance, and all the rivers give homage and attest to his grandeur and glory. Nawsoo nhawros ha shem, nawsoo nhawros kolum—the torrid oceans and the stormy seas give way. The swift fury of the sea gives way and becomes calm before the awesome fearful word of G-d. This is the song of Deborah which also personifies the ideas of sublimating and transforming nature to the will of G-d. Not to serve nature, rather to expose nature and the entire physical world into the spirituality of G-d. The idea of sheviras hakailim—of transposing nature into the sublime, spiritual element, reducing the finite into the infinite, wreaking through the mundane material world and extracting from it the refined, ethical principle of ultimate spirituality unto Almighty G-d is the ecstatic response of Israel to G-d upon vindicating them and championing them from the harsh slavery, the misery and misfortune that they experienced in Egypt. Shirah, poetry liberates the soul and gives an ecstatic experience to those who are engulfed in bondage, immersed in slavery for decades and centuries. Hashamayim m'saprim kevod El umase yawdovmagid haw rawkeeoh—the heavens and the earth tell the tale of the glory of G-d. They recite his accomplishment and give cognizance to the Great, the Tremendous, and Ineffable one. Vhoo kchawsun yotzai maichoopusoh—The strength of the sun is inestimable, immeasurable. However this adornment of nature and this ecstatic response to the grandeur and luster and beauty of sublimating nature, the emotional understanding of nature must be harmonized and infused with the law of G-d. Nature, and the entire physical world, the material strata of the world is but a frame for the diamond and immense immeasurable value of the Torah. Vain nistur maichamawsaw—no one is concealed, no one can escape, no one can flee from the tremendous exposure of nature, from the grasp of G-d's glory, molo kul haaretz kvodo. However this emotional outpour of uzyushir, of the ecstatic experience of exodus is realized only against the background of toras hashem tmimah. G-d's law is perfect and the fulfillment of His precepts is the only essence wherein men can flourish. Exodus is a prelude to maimood har sinai.

There are two steps, two classic dramas that Israel witnessed upon its formation on becoming a nation, yitzeeos mitzraim and maimood har sinai. In both there is the classic phrase of Reeyaw-Vyaar Yisroel es hayod hagdolaw asher awsaw Hashem b'mitz-rayim. Israel saw the mighty hand, the great wonders, the miraculous intervention that G-d bestowed upon Israel to uplift them from the mire of misery, to eradicate that ugly yoke of bondage that engulfs man like a vise upon his neck robbing him of his tzelem Elokim of his unique spiritual image, striving for G-dly perfection. So Israel saw the great wonder, the reality of G-d, where G-d came to battle with Egypt, the war of G-d Ha shem Ish milchomaw to expose the material quest of Egypt, of Mitzrayim, that finite hold upon man that seeks to chain him and contain him, that seeks to oppress and to trample upon man's great dignity, upon the divine image that has been inspired in him. However, the great natural wonder that G-d demonstrated to Israel cannot rest alone, for G-d, is not merely a ruler in time of bondage. G-d comes to Israel with a message of Ehye asher Ehye, that the idea of continuity is to prevail, cultural creativity must continue. However, when can this idea off spirituality become the unique historic heritage of Israel? Only if there is a matan torah, a vchol hawam royim eshakolos—the people witnessed the aseres hadibros. They saw the intellectual creativity of G-d's precepts, they attested to the great event of cultural creativity, that freedom is predicated upon the principle of cultural and intellectual performance, of learning and study. This is the idea of freedom. It is not a reckless abandonment of a yoke. Rather, it is designed to give man the sense of responsibility and a feeling of dignity. After Egypt was destroyed and submerged in the sea Israel was confronted by Amalek, who came and fought with her. Moses told Joshua to select men to go and do battle and fight the Amalekites, and Joshua routed the Amalekites and Moses therein built an altar and called it, G-d is my flag, my eternal salvation. For it is an everlasting battle unto G-d to eradicate Amalek from the seat of world civilization. What is the idea and what is the contrast of these two confrontations, namely with Egypt and Amalek? Is there any distinction that one can raise between the two encounters? Furthermore, there are two parsheeos in Bshalach and Keesay tzay, two recountings of the story and battle of Amalek. In one portion—write this as an everlasting memory in a book. For I shall uproot and eradicate the memory of Amalek-kee mowcho emcher—and in another portion we read, and it shall come to be when G-d shall give you requite from your enemies, then you shall uproot and eradicate the memory of Amalek from the earth-timche. In Bshalach G-d assures, and gives his word that he shall annihilate and destroy the vicious Amalek who tried to ensnare the Israelites, who tried by devious and deceptive means to cut away, to tear asunder the dignity of Israel when they were moving forward from that miraculous feat of Exodus. Amalek entered upon a deceptive plan while the Jews were fatigued. On route Amalek tried cunningly to corrupt and to falsify the legitimate claim of Israel's unique sovereign historic message. In Kee saytsay however we find that the Jews are commanded and compelled by G-d to go out and do battle with Amalek. It is their responsibility to uproot, eliminate, annihilate and eradicate Amalek. Why the two conflicting reports? They seem to contradict one another. If G-d has assured and promised that Amalek shall be uprooted, why is there a need for a commandment, why is it necessary to be commanded. What is the idea of the precept if there is a promise? There are two kinds of battles that confront the historic quest for fulfilling the Jewish sovereign message and convey Israel's unique mission to the world. They are accomplished by two means, namely passive and active. After Egypt had suffered so many plagues why did they seek to encounter Israel on the Red Sea? Because Egypt thought that G-d is fighting their war in a passive manner. True the plagues came upon Egypt. However it is only because of G-d's will that Israel should be submissive, passive, and obedient to the will of G-d. However, when he came to the sea, when he confronted Israel in war, there he thought man to man he will be able to conquer and to overwhelm Israel, that G-d will only perform miracles in a passive manner. However, in an actual military conquest Egypt is unbeatable, no power can conquer Egypt in battle. It is only through the passive submissive aspect that nature somehow intervenes. This was the idea of Pharaoh's pursuit. That actively he could conquer Israel. The reason for the plagues was because Israel is only victorious in a passive way. Israel cannot command itself in battle. G-d says to Moses Ma titzokaylai? why scream unto me, why do prayer? Now is a time for movement, for traveling, for speedy escape. The battle of Egypt, the Exodus, came about through a passive, submissive adherence unto G-d Moses says to Israel—HaShem yi lochaym lawchem Vatem tachareeshoon—G-d will do your battles, G-d will conquer Egypt and you will stand aside in a silent manner. You will be a silent partner watching the great feat, the great miracles of G-d. Amalet was cognizant of this fact and he tried by deceptive and cunning methods to uproot Israel in a sneak attack. Israel would not be aware of Amalek's venture. Israel would be caught napping. Brefeedim, as the Rabbis comment, rufooyudom, their hands are tired, they are tired. They don't think anyone is foolish enough to intervene and do battle with them, to try and encounter them on the battlefield. So Amalek continues the battle in an active way and Moses commands Joshua that there is another way of perpetuating the historic message. That is then a nation comes upon us in a deceptive and deceitful way, we must do battle with them, uproot them, and annihilate them from the face of the earth. Amalek has no right to sit, to take its proper seat amidst the council of nations. Her sovereignty must be conquered, challenged, and encountered on the battlefield. There are many wars in Tanach, some were conquered in a passive way as we know from the battle of Sanchereb and Cheskiah. Sanchereb was defeated by the angel of G-d, pestilence came upon his military camp and in one moment, in a striking occurrence, Sanchereb was cut asunder from the military scene of world civilization. He was torn away from his gigantic military feats and his tremendous exploits on the battlefield. He was put to shame, to everlasting scorn. There are other battles however where the Jews must participate in an active way because the nations of the world try by deceit and cunning to uproot and annihilate them. This is seen in the war with Median and Balak who contrived to eradicate the Jewish community by luring them to the beauty, lustful to the eternal glamour, to the outward glow of their civilization and culture. They tried to make the Jews turn from G-d and pursue their passions and lust for the Medianite women. By praising their beautiful tents, Bilum sought to make the Jews enamored of external beauty, of the glamour and glitter in becoming seduced and lured to the Medanite culture. Therefore G-d says: Tzror es ha Midyonim—to pursue the Medanites in battle and to annihilate them, because they try by cunning and devious methods to uproot you. Pharaoh and Sannechereb tried to conquer the Jews by military exploits of that day and age. It was no unique kind of strategy. It was only because of their might that they challenged G-d. So G-d intervened. Amalek and Bilum challenged Israel. Israel must come out of ts shell, must break through the ivory tower and demonstrate to the world that they are actively involved and they can convey both intellectually and militarily their historic heritage. When is there a commandment and precept on the intellectual plane? When Israel is confronted with its unique historic sovereignty, when its destiny is being challenged they must go out to war: Vawloo mosheeim b'ltar Zion lishpot es Har Esuv. The great leaders, the redeemers of Israel shall go up from the mountain of Zion to judge and conquer the mountain of Esuv. The assurance of mawcho emche is in the broader physical aspect—that is militarily Amalek will be subdued ultimately. The precept conveys the task of our own assertion in the spiritual domain that Zion shall tower above Esuv. Judaism and Hellenism are locked in an historic battle. And moreover, Judaism has been locked in battle with all the civilizations of the world; with Egypt and Canaan—keemaasay Eretz Mitzra m Kee maaseh canaan lo Soasoo—teh abominations, and the evils of Canaan you should not engage in, in their atrocities you should not participate. Mizraim presents to Israel the challenge of enduring within slavery, of prevailing within servitude, within the dire Mezer of Egypt, with the quantified restrictive atmosphere and asphyxiating environment of Egypt Israel must endure. Canaan presents another kind of civilization—beauty, economic material luster, and the splendor of the high fashion social life. When you are a sovereign nation you should not go astray seeking the beauty and the niceties of Canaan, their fancy ways and their great lust for fashion, for etiquette and the external glamour and outward glitter of their civilization. You should not adorn yourself in their attire, n their mode of pagan living. Their dress covers their abominations. You should not cloth yourself and enrapture yourself in the garment that rakes your soul, uproots your cultural identity.

Now Jethro also observed the great wonder, the miraculous feats that G-d performed for Israel. And Jethro understands and appreciates the great glory of G-d. He declared: "Blessed is G-d who saved and redeemed Israel from the Oppressive yoke of Egypt." He does not seek to lure and trap, and ensmare like Bilum. Rather his conception of Israel is the attempt to reconcile their problems with the general community. The question is apparent, why was Jethro responsible for the parshah of reeataw secheze—that is when Moses was tiring from judging Israel from morning till night Jethro complained to Moses and explained to him that he can't go on with such a procedure. He must alter his course as a jurist lest he shall become weary and will no longer be able to fulfill and perform aptly in his service as leader of the nation. Why is Jethro so concerned? What is his reason for explaining to Moses the need for gradation in judges, for judges who can judge the multitudes, judges that are selected for unique cases, and finally if there is a quarrel a litigation that no one can render proper decision then and only then shall they come before you.

There is something perhaps that is inherent in Jethro's own character that enables him to contribute this important message to Moses, "Vataw sechze lom hazeh anshe chayil vsonay bawtzar." You shall see and it shall become your task to appoint and nominate judges who are courageous and bold, judges who disdain material gain, judges who have a love of truth and yearn for justice, who crave for the legal order, for the legal norm. In Jethro's praising of G-d he declares "Blessed is G-d who is greater than all the other gods upon the earth." Jethro in his own theological conception assumed a hierarchy of supernatural beings, perhaps angels, perhaps seraphim. Jethro therefore was able to transform and transpose his theological conceptions into a legal system and a proper judicial order. Jethro is the one who characteristically conveys to Moses the message of a judicial hierarchy, because he was always imbued with this idea. Jethro does not seek to pure Moses to the Midianite cult like Bilum. Jethro rather seeks to contribute to the legislative and judicial order of Israel. This is why Moses in *Numbers* asks and requests of Jethro that he might go along with them in the arduous journey of the kilderness for he is responsible and concerned with the welfare and security of the Jewish community, not like Bilum, his counterpart, the prophet of Median, the visionary who attempts to ensnare and entrap Judaism in the beauty and luster of idolatrous heathendom. Jethro on the contrary seeks to extract and carve out a social order from his theological conception and presenting it to the Jewish community that they might be able to know the path of G-d and to perform the actions that are so necessary in creating a more perfect society.

The Ten Commandments, the decalogue, is the blueprint upon which the entire structure of legal norms; civil, criminal, social, personal, folkways and mores are carved out hewed from the rocks. From the stones of the shay loochos ha brith we carve, we form the great and prodigious, the luminous, multiferous legal code that has been commented and expounded upon for millenia. What is it which characterizes this code? What does it present for us? What is the lesson for continuity, the morality of a timeless heritage for a timeless people that has come down to us from aseres hadibros, from the classic event of Sinai?

The Decalogue represents that true relationship for man; that perfect harmony between man's private, personalized and particularized maturation and the total general public life to which he must convey his identity contributing to the communal well being and enhancing the security of society, advancing thereby a vibrant dynamic Jewish life. There are two documents, as it were, that we have in the Decalogue. In Jethro we read, "Remember the day of Sabbath. It is a rest day for

G-d, for when He conceived of the creation of this earth, he consummated it with a day of rest." Hence the symbol of G-d's serenity is consecrated and sanctified within the Sabbath. Zchor es yom hashabbas lkadsh, remember the day of the Sabbath in sanctity, to consecrate time and dedicate oneself to the concept of hallowing G-d through the ongoing process of one's ultimate commitment to him, through the idea of the spiritual sublime serenity that is indicative in Sabbath. Nature, therefore, is sublimated and transformed into a peaceful, blissful, serene beauty, dignity, and majesty. Yyawnoch ba yom Hasheveeee. Then we have another idea of Sabbath, another Divine concept. That is, in order for everyone to rest there shall no longer be bondage or servitude as there was in Egypt. Spiritual rest is inextricably intertwined with a rest from physical toil, with a stoppage of the regular daily movement, and to turn from the chol, from the weekday to a new, a revived day that is designed to uplift, elevate, consecrate, and dedicate man to a more sublime spiritual existence realizing thereby his Creator and fulfilling therein his image of G-dliness.

The idea of Shabbas, the sanctity of the Sabbath is followed by the commandment of honoring the parents, honoring the mishpocheh, the family from which you are nurtured. Why does the commandment of Kabel esawveechaw ves eemechaw precede the ommandment of Shabbas? Sim larly in Kdoshim we read eesh emo vaviv teero ves shabsosgi tishmoroo oomi kdawshee tirohoo ahnee Ha Shem—that feat of parents is predicated on the idea of observance of Sabbath. There is a certain nexus between sustaining the purity of family life, the sanctity of family life with the sanctity of Sabbath. Why? What is the relationship between the two precepts? How does fulfillment of one bring about the acquisition of the other?

When a person is nurtured in an environment of supreme religious feeling, complete spiritual dedication, then he worships, values, and understands the idea of spiritual serenity. Likewise the sanctity of time that is implicit in the Sabbath is a prerequisite and a precondition to the sanctity of time that is represented and expressed in the generations of family life. Thus the family and the Sabbath are intertwined in a revival of the body, a continuity of the spirit. The family gives physical continuity; the Sabbath rejuvenates one with spiritual continuity. Then the precepts, the prohibitions against conniving, conceit, stealing, plundering your fellow men is understood against the background of a pure religious development. When he is reared and his being is established within the context of an environment that gives one growth and development in the spiritual sense with the meaning of sanctity then the property of his fellow man, the person of his fellow man assumes a new meaning, a meaning of holiness. One comes to a relationship with his fellow man with a feeling of holiness, sanctity. Therefore Kdoshim teeyew kee kawdosh anee—G-d expresses the idea that Israel shall become sanctified when their life is predicated on the principle of dedicating themselves to the supreme task of sanctity. And sanctity is no small matter that comes about lightly. One must assert himself with complete vigor and with a great amount of fortitude to aspire to this concept of kee dooshau Tookad aish—sanctity is a contraction of two words, a flaming fire. Man must sublimate and transform the fire and zeal of his energy, capacity for lust, greed, power, strength and channelize these energies and drives motivating them for a useful creative productive purpose. The fire, therefore, that is within man to rule, to conquer, must be transformed into the fire of enhancing the path and advancing the road to guide him along the rugged, curving, twisting trail, journey and voyage in whatever avenue of life he finds himself, in whatever place he is in whatever circumstance. Kawdosh is the fire that man expresses, the emotion, drive, energy, and fervor that he channels to the direction of devotion and dedication unto Almighty G-d.

Thus Nadav and Aveehoo were cut asunder and torn away because they brought forth the strange fire aishzarah, asher lo tzoovaisee, that I have not commanded. They did not properly channel their emotions. True, they intended to bring and make their sacrifice, to consecrate themselves. However, it was not with the will and desire that G-d had commanded. They had great potential, tremendous amount of energy; however, it was not channeled and directed or motivated in the way that G-d required. Therefore haloklol divorai kaish noom Ha Shem oochfataishy fotzaitz selah—my words are like a flaming fire and like a hammer splitting rocks, driving man away from his passions, lust, and hot pursuit after vain pleasure, material splendor, economic affluence and abundance that he endeavors to multiply. How then can kdosshaw be fostered? In what environment must it be established, nurtured, developed, and how do we maintain and continue this concept of Kedooshaw and taharah? This is possible and feasible if there is a place wherein Kedooshaw is centered. Aizeh bayis asher tivneh lee—how can one build a house as it were for Al-mighty G-d, and how can we establish a house, a place, a geographically limited and finite boundary wherein man can conceive of G-d. Mlo kol haaretz kvodo, how can one confine the sublime spiritual fire of G-d within a limited place? How can the Al-mighty One be conseived of and contemplated within the context and concept if physical dimension? How can we make the ain sof enter into a place which is only limited by spacial dimensions. Only G-d can answer that vasoo lee mikdosh vshechantee besochum, that man can consecrate and dedicate G-d not only in the midbar away from civilization, remote from communal life, and far removed from the mainstream of social intercourse. G-d does not merely dwell in the wilderness. The G-d that extricated Israel from bondage and servitude, to lead them through the Midbar through the arid torrid desert is not merely a G-d that dwells in the wilderness. He is not only a loner away from civilization. Rather he is the G-d who can dwell within the miskkan, within the house of beauty, within an environment of majestic wealth and splendor. The idea of G-dliness is all embracing, Kol makom asher azkeer es shimee avoailedia oovairachteechaw. G-d, wherever one mentions Him, that is where he is found. This is the function of the miskan. It was made with precious skins, ornamented with silver and gold and adorned with the most costly material products, designed with architectural skill and developed with immense precision because we have to convey this message, communicate this mission to the world at large: G-d does not merely dwell in the forest away from world civilization. He does not call unto his prophets merely from the burning bush where no one but the prophet can see G-d. He calls to Israel from the ohel moed. True, there are singular, elite men who hear the call of G-d in the mid-bar, in the lonely twilight, in the darkness of night, in the dense loneliness that is far removed. They have a certain sublime task. There is a mission of the midbar and the forest is for them, the rendezvous where they contact G-d. However, there is also a vnoadetee where G-d conveys his message of celestial spiritual sanctity in the ohel moed, before everyone. There is a meeting place where all can appreciate, can ascertain the idea of G-dliness. This is expressed in the character of Jacob, soolum mootzuv arzaw crosho mageeah hasha maimaw, like a ladder which is set straight on the ground and yet reaches up above. There are those that reach up above, they are in the tower crosho mageeah sha maimaw—they are in the ivory tower, way up on top of the mountain. Moshe awlaw el hahar and Israel besachtis hahar. Moses went up to the mount, Moses could climb the summit of supreme, religious and spiritual attainment, Moses can ascend to the sublime ultimate and to obtain the plateau of understanding G-d on the mountain. Far away, there is truly a place for the gigantic creative leader at the mountain, in the wilderness, or in the forest, away, far removed, remotely disengaged from the community. However, this greatness of creativity, this tremendous development of one's own personal growth is not to be divorced, disassociated or disconnected from the community at large. Rather it must be reconciled, harmonized, infused within the total dimension of expressing the cognizance of G-4, the intellectual idea and the creative theology that is inherent in G-d, in the understanding of Him. There is miskan and there is mikdosh. One idea of miskan is a dwelling place for Israel themselves to express greatness of glory, grandeur and the beauty and flow of G-d to the particular lamechaw private community of Israel, oovchain tain kovod Ha Shem, only for Israel, for we have our own sacred and unique mission to perform. However, there is a mikdosh for the world kee baisee bais tefilaw yee koray lchol haamim. My house shall be considered as a house of worship for the entire world. Ndeevai amim nesophoo am Elohai Avraham. The princes of the nations have gathered together. They are the people of the G-d of Abraham. Therefore, there is a particular community of miskan and also the universal community of bikdosh. The Gemorah declares: Miskan and Mikdosh are inextricably intertwined. Within the contexts of mishkan we have a commandment of constructing a shemen zayis zuch—to illuminate an incandescent light for His dwelling place. And you shall command Aaron that he should erect the light. Why do we insert the precept of making the light from the shemen, from olive oil? Within mishkan we see G-d's Majesty, His beauty reigning with glory and His covereignty is expressed in a magnificent splendor. G-d's reign is attired in a material fashion that is incomparable, with precious skins, silver, gold, all kinds of materials that are designed in the fashioning of the mishkan. However, when the zayis zach, the olive is beaten down, struck down we then extract and exude more oil, finer oil, more fragrant oil. The zayis reminds us of Israel's historic mission throughout the two millenia of misery and misfortune wherein they have encompassed pogroms, pillaging and plundering by the nations of the world, and inversely proportionate to their suffering they have endured with a triumphal success in shaping their destiny and contributing to their creative Jewish spiritual leadership not only in their cultural milieu, but also for the entire world civilization. The zayis zach—the one who was beaten, crushed down, trampled upon is the one that gives radiance and incandescent luminating light to the entire world about us. As we have stated previously od yosaif chaivchee hoo moshel bchol Mitzrayim. Joseph who was thrust aside, cast into the pit was miraculously elevated to the plateau where he could express his genius of contribution and creative leadership, not only for his brethren, but also for Egypt. Not only is he the parshah symbolizing malchoos—leadership, glory for his nation, he is also the symbol of the dynamic force in Egyptian civilization. Similarly, Moses, Joshua, and David, and all the other Jewish leaders who were great in Judea, were equally revered and respected throughout the entire world.

We read in the portions of Trumab and Ttsavah vlo vasoor habadim mayal haaron vlo yeezach hachoshun maydl haayfor—about the entire movement and journey of the mishkan where we have construction and destruction, great periods of peaceful, blissful, cultural continuity, and on the other hand, epics of destruction, ensuing peril, enduring suffering. Nevertheless, there is an havtuchah, an assurance form Al-mihty G-d that although the mishkan is in ruin vahasheemosee es mikdoshee, although the holy places lay desolate and decimated, nevertheless they retain their spiritual purity and serve as a reflection for enduring historic time. Throughout our transient historic travail in all our experiences in nationhood we have never been removed from the arena of cultural creativity. We have always participated and made our indelible imprint with our cultural giants and spiritual heroes. From Babylonia to Spain, from France to Germany, from Russia to Poland, to here on shores of the U.S.A. we have a heroic march, depicted in the Mishna of Kaylimesser golooyos gulsa shechina—that the Divine inspiration, the Divination within Israel has experienced ten exiles. We may paraphrase it in our own historic time: that we have again returned to the birthplace of our homeland. Kee rabimbnay shomaymaw meb-nay boolaw—Many are the children of the desolate one, of the decimated one from the one who is economically fruitful, from the one who is materially successful. In our masoretic drama we have contributed above and beyond the call of history and the mission of Israel remains supreme, the goals of Judah are retained to its unparalleled plateau, and the zeal of Zion is renewed, rejuvenated and invigorated with a new zest, a new fortitude, and a new age in a new period, in a new epic of unequalled material splendor, economic affuence, and technical abundance of goods. In this era of great material success man seeks to create for himself images of pride, golden statues of lust, and vain idolatrous gods of glory. This passion is filled with an unsurpassed fury, with an immeasurable thirst for greed and envy. Therefore he designs for himself an egel haxahav—molten image to express his might, his power. He creates images to exploit others, religious symbols though they may appear to the public are just methods and means to exploit others and rape the public with spiritual deceit. Moses the champion of our historic heritage comes to klal yisroel from the mountain. He descends and when he reaches the camp of Israel seeing how they are immersed in their lustful pride of casting an image, Moses grasps the golden calf and smashes it. This is the greatness of Moses, to smash the idolatrous images of lust and pride that man creates for himself to exploit and take advantage of others. This is what Moses cries out against. This is the mission Moses. In an age of so much technical superiority man moves away from the idea of G-dliness and slides back into the pitfalls of spiritual abyss, becomes void of his cultural heritage, and vacuum ensues, a vacuum of material lust, greed, pride and envy encompasses his being. Therefore Moses has to break the idol, to extricate Israel from the plight of becoming subdued to a new kind of slavery, engulfed in the bondage of his own vain power, of his great fury for lust and passion, of his steaming drive for greed, of his anxiety for conquest. From this bondage Moses also seeks to extricate Israel, Moses cry, plea and supplication into G-d is: Have you only extricated us from physical bondage so that we may become newly enslaved to a new kind of slavery, that is to our own material power. That we do not have the cultural desire, nor do we have the spiritual drive to fulfill the mission of our forefathers. Zchor l'Avraham lyitzchok, l'yaacov—Remember the covenant of Abraham, Isaac, and Jacob, that we have a mission to perform and we have a task. We have a goal to exercise to preserve the heritage of our forefathers, and to continue the goals of G-dliness. Therefore, Moses prays to G-d that Israel shall be inextricably intertwined with Almighty G-d so that they may never exceed the bounds of their material power and become enslaved to their passions, in servitude to their vain and futile desires. Tefilay le Moshe or vayetar yitzchok—prayer binds Israel with Al-mighty G-d. As Israel or anyone cannot escape from G-d—Hayisoser eech bamistorim vanee lo erenoo—can one conceal himself in the clefts of the crevices and I, Almighty G-d, will not see him, cannot observe him? Who can come in the cracks of the slopes of the mountains, who can hide mipnay pachad hadargono—before the fury and awesome glory of Almighty G-d? No one can escape from the power, from the image of G-d. Tfilah from the root of taf like tfeesah, grasps hold of G-d as it were, so that we will not be forever forsaken, that we shall bind the Almighty One to us like one being, attired and adorned in His splendor. That is the semantic identification with vayeter atarah—prayer is the crown of G-d, the crown of His glory and the apex of His eternal splendor. Although G-d is filled with wrath against Israel's spiritual descent into the pitfalls of abyss, nevertheless the great leader, the one who is filled with majestic character and attired with the noble and divine inspiration can bind and intertwine G-d with Israel. The navee expresses this idea vtomar Zion azavanee ha Shem vHa Shem she shaychonee—that the L-rd has forsaken and forgotten us and we are forlorn, there is no hope, no salvation, and no redemption. G-d answers that just as a woman can't forget her children so will I never forsake you. Only for a moment have I scorned you, but with great mercy, with great compassion, and with great concern shall I come to restore your glory as of old, shall I extricate you from the plight of spiritual dilemma, of spiritual doubt. This is the formula for anee ldodee vdodee lee—that there is a bond, an interconnecting rope that shall never fall, a rope that remains ever tied, ever knotted between Israel and G-d. Yisroel varaisaw koodsha breechoo chad—The timeless message of Israel's mission is everlasting and unique. Thus *Exodus* is the story of Israel's liberation from two categories of bondage, one from the enslavement of Egypt and also from their own internal servitude becoming enslaved to the passions and lust of their material splendor. There are two kinds of troomah, two ways in which a man offers his material plenty, of which G-d has enriched him with great economic affluence. Koleesh asher gidvenoo lebo and hausheer lo yarve whadal lo yamit. The donation of the silver half piece is regulated and precise. The silver coin must be given equally by all. There is a kind of religious expression that must be regulated, structured, no more, no less, a specific stipulation. That is perhaps to counteract external rigidity that seeks to ensnare man and encroach upon him to quantify him. Therefore the Torah realized that man must have some legal structural form wherein he could apply his self-expression and fulfill himself by regulating the spiritual tax of his material wealth. However, there is another manner wherein the Torah realized that a person is filled with emotion and he wants to feel some elation, some exuberance over the fact that he has attained material splendor because he has ascertained a certain measure and degree of affluence. Therefore the Torah tells him that he might donate what he desires—asher yidvenoo lebo. *Exodus* is the symbol of liberation from those internal frustrations, internal problems, internal dilemmas that seek to ensnare, to entrap, and to encroach upon man. Also there are external phenomena that swoop down upon man and surround him from all angles, from all areas, from all boundary lines. They fasten their vulgar lid upon his freedom of thought, freedom of ethical expression, freedom of his supreme desire to attain the sublime religious experience. That is the idea of chayroot. As the Rabbis expressed it chayroot is ayn lchaw elaw mee sheosek batorah—the one who is involved in ideas the one who is immersed in a Torah living life is truly a free person. Choroos al ha loochos—"Do not read choroos (carving), read chayroos, read freedom." Engraved in the loochos was this unique idea of freedom. That to be liberated from the yoke of bondage is not a license for licentiousness. Rather it presupposes a certain responsibility that man is destined to go beyond his physical needs, his material wants and to reach out beyond the external environment of glamor and glitter and to overcome his pride and passion.

Sheal neawlechaw meal roglechaw kee ha mawkom asher ataw omaid a lux admas kodesh hoo—Remove your shoes from your feet for this land whereupon you stand is a land of holiness, a land of sanctity, a land of supreme spiritual fervor. It gushes forth with the emotion of G-dliness. K-d calls to Moses from the burning bush to strip himself from his material pride. His ambition to become a leader can only be realized if he divorces himself from this desire. That only if G-d calls, that is when he becomes a leader, laych rayd migdooluschaw—Go down, descend from your power because Israel has sinned and if Israel has committed an atrocity you have no right, you have no privilege to be a leader, you have no power as a leader, you have no pride in being a commander of Israel. If they sinned, the burden of guilt is upon you and the responsibility of blame is upon your shoulders. Cloom nsatee lchaw gdoolaw elaw bishvil yisroel. "Only because of Israel have I given you the honor of standing before me. Now depart from my countenance," declares G-d Ayl Rachoom v'chanoon—that prayer is the ultimate way wherein wan leads back, comes back to G-d. Of course prayer must be rooted with Torah, with law, with study. They are inextricably intertined, mishpatim and mishkan—the law and the dwelling place of spirituality are intertwined. Kdooshah must be predicated upon a system of law. The continuity of kdooshah can only be realized against the background and environment of intellectual attainment of spirituality. "Ayn boor yraychayt vlo amhaaretz chasid," declared the Sages. An ignorant person cannot have reverence for G-d nor can he excel in piety, nor can he worship G-d properly if he has not the intellectual imagination, creativity to worship G-d, to reach out over his mundane material world and to grasp, to catch hold of Shechina. Therefore mishkan proceeds mishpatim—the dwelling place of kdooshah must be nurtured and fostered upon the foundation of law. Zichras Toras Moshe avdee and mismor sheer chanookas ha bays l'Dovid—The bayisl' Dovid can only be built after we have Toras Moshe, after one has dedicated his life on the fundation of the Torah.

Then we can have mloochaw kingship. Oobay hayawlas ha awnun al homiskkan—Only when the cloud of shechinah would ascend on the tabernacle, then only could Moses be able to enter into the mishkan. Moses cannot so easily enter mishkan. Moses himself can come into kdooshaol only if he has the license and the permission from Almighty G-d. He can be an architect, a leader, a magistrate, a commander. However into mishkai he can only come if G-d allows him. If G-d calls unto Moses, Vyikrael Moshe—then he can come into kdooshah, shal nalechaw mayal raglechaw is the rendezvous point wherein G-d calls and makes his encounter to Moses. Strip yourself from your luster, from your pride. Oomoshe lo yawda bdabro eethee koran or pawnaf—Moses himself was not aware when he had spoken to the people that his face was lustered, adorned, and attired in an expression of radiance, in an exuberant splendor of/or light that emanates intellectually and creatively.

When Moses assembled the people to declare that the mishkan had been erected, established, constructed, he warns them and admonishes them that there should not be any fire on Sabbath. As we know this is explicitly prohibited in the Torah.

To acquire complete spiritual fulfillment, one should abstain from physical toil or any labor that is enjoined in the Torah. This has been expressly delegated to the Rabbis as to how they may interpret the definition of mlawchaw—what constitutes a desecration and violation of work on Sabbath. There is another kind of malacha that has been expressly prohibited in the Torah and that is carrying any object from one domain, from one's private area to the thoroughfare or in the thoroughfare itself. One must not carry an article from rshoos harabim to rshoos hayawcheed. Thus we have two classes of work, two malachos that have been expressly defined as forbidden in the Torah. Why these two? Lighting a fire symbolizes creativity in work, a quantative change of matter, new elements. Man's power to create, to form, to shape has been forbidden and prohibited on Sabbath. This lust for molding matter, man's desire and eagerness to transform the elements, to demonstrate his capacity that he is a creative domineering being has been put to rest on Sabbath. It has ceased, for Sabbath is the day of spiritual serenity that is devoid of man's ambition for demonstrating his capacity of creative work. Rather, on this day man should demonstrate his ability to be a spiritual being, that almighty G-d has created the world, that he should be cognizant of his fellow man, as he was a servant in Egypt and he was freed. Likewise, must he free himself and liberate his being from servitude of material splendor, of being in bondage to material lust, material want, and material gain. On this day man is to act passive, placid and pleasant. Sabbath is therefore designated in our liturgy as chemdas hayomim, the most beautiful of days. An instrument of pleasantness as the Torah klee chemdas is called likewise is Sabbath depicted as a day of pleasant, peaceful serenity where manccan experience a sublime, blissful, spiritual existence, devoid of the rush and push of every day life where he is called upon, to be an active, thriving, moving, mobile being. On this day he is passive, he surrenders his being unto G-d, recognizing that there is a higher calling beyond his everyday struggle of mere subsistence for his daily bread and existence for the lust, passion, and pride that vulgarizes his being and strips him of attaining spiritual goals, of becoming elevated in reaching a higher ethical plateau in life. Not to be subservient to his own works, to what he has fashioned, made, and designed, rather to become a person who recognizes there is something above and beyond the six days of toil. And on this day when we shall experience a Sabbath for humanity. For Shabbas is designated as the malkah, as the queen. Shabbas is depicted as the queen who is passive, beautiful, adorned in splendid attire, garbed in glamorous garments thereby expressing a new kind of relationship to man liberating his soul. Man can transform and sublimate his passion and pride that aim to vulgarize and make him subservient. Sabbath can extricate him from the bondage of material servitude by a new uplifting, by realizing that the queen of material splendor has been transformed into the princess of celestial placidness, that it has been sublimated into a majestic beauty of the Shabbas malkah. Herein lies his pride, herein lies his beauty where all his toil must be aimed, motivated, directed, to the goal of hadar spiritual bliss, spiritual pride, spiritual adornment. Then there is another category of work that has been expressly prohibited in the Torah, and that is carrying an object from one's private domain into the thoroughfare. Herein the Torah explicitly prohibited a qualitative change in work, in active, daily work. There is quality transforming from a private dominion to the community dominion. There is an abstract concept that we may infer from this prohibition, that man is forbidden to abstractify and conceptualize in a manner that will bring him to a mundane materialized, corruptive and corrosive character. Abstraction is the highest form of man's intellectual capacity for attainment to the spiritual and ethical goals that lead him to the ultimate plateau of dvaykoos, cleaving unto G-d. Ethics, morals, the soonim bunim of life must be predicated on an intellectual and creative plateau. Mishkan has to be rooted in mishpatim. Beauty, majesty, the ornamentation of material splendor has to be shaped, formed and designed in an abstract concept that leads man above and directs him beyond material goals, material aims, material drives. Man therefore is commanded that he must rest on Sabbath for then he will realize the abstract relationship, the abstract understanding the abstract identification with G-d.

Exodus is therefore the book that provides man with the ecstatic experience of liberating himself from all kinds of bondage, from all types of servitude that tend to engulf man and deceive him away from the path of the spiritual road. *Exodus* gives man the root, shows him the root of walking in the wilderness and the root of dwelling in the Tabernacle. Man, whatever his endeavor may be must be able to adapt to the circumstances however difficult, however tormenting they tend to be. He must snap the yoke of bondage and break the burdening cruel shackling chains of slavery. This is the anun, the cloud and fire that goes through the midbar to show the Jew the way. The fire of sublimating man's passions into that form that will lead him to a more spiritual form that will show the way, guideposts of religiosity that is the symbol of the amood haanun, the cloud of fire that ascends on the tent of the lhelmoayd, the cloud of glory that directs man the way to go.

LEVITICUS

Chapter 3

There are two classes of sacrifice wherein man dedicates his material wealth unto G-d and he delivers of his personal gain to be sacrificed on the altar, on the G-dly altar wherein man sublimates his material wealth and transforms it into a spiritual service. There are worbonos such as the olaw, minchaw, shelomim. That is man seeks to elevate himself when he offers a present unto G-d, in seeking spiritual perfection by offering of his material gain, his material wealth, not to boast and be prideful of his economic affluence, not to brag about his powerful economic exploits, about his riches. Rather man uses his material prosperity in a cultural and spiritual fashion. When man sins and defiles his divine character, when he slips to the abyss of spiritual demoralization and degradation, then he offers the sin offering, the chatus, the awshem after which he becomes again elevated unto G-d. Hence we find sacrifices that are of a perfecting nature, that seek to make man a perfect being, to either elevate him from his mediocre status or to uplift him from his sinful position. However these sacrifices are of progress, they denote man's attempt for spiritual, cultural, ethical progress. This is the man of everyday life, the average person who has attained spiritual or cultural prestige or has attained material and economic wealth. Whatever rung on the ladder of society he has attained, whatever posture in the social structure he has attained, these sacrifices seek only to perfect and to compliment his relationship unto G-d. There is however another status of sacrifice wherein man's whole being, his total, collective personality is even at times persecuted from within, internal insurgence into his very system that uproot his character, that make him crushed, his character is stricken by external forces, by external problems, by external dilemmas. There is a man who is on the lowest level or has been crushed from without and down-trodden, depressed, and despondent and distraught, wherein he cannot be on an equal level, on an equal standing with his fellow man in the community. He is the destitute, meek and deprived. For that there is another class of worbunos. The korban sacrifice of the mtzoral, the leper or the zuv, the one who has certain types of excretions and even the woman who has given birth, she who has born a child brings an offering, for who knows what the child will be, whether he will realize his potential, whether he will realize his potential, whether he will ascertain to the spiritual heights of G-dliness, or will sink into the mire of spiritual abyss. Who know what can happen to the person in all walks of life? Who knows what occurs and who knows to what circumstances life can expose the human character to situations that are unfathomable, inestimable and immeasurable? There is another sacrifice wherein man dedicates his ultimate being unto G-d with a contrite spirit, when his whole being is crushed and persecuted. Min hamaytzar karawsee yaw, awnawnee bamerchav yaw. Out of the depths of struggle, anguish, strife and agony comes the cry of the religious person who is crushed from without and crippled from within and cannot reach out to anyone. Almighty G-d can only answer him. There are the worbonas that are wrought when man is afflicted with negoyim, with plagues of all types, when the Jewish nation was confronted with pogroms of all sorts, when they were afflicted, persecuted, plundered, and pillaged from without, ransacked and raped from within. This is another cry, one of min hamaytzar.

We can give some plausible explanation to the problem of the aytz hadas. When man sinned against G-d, when he ate from the tree of knowledge, he knew of the difference between right and wrong. How can there be a chote nizkeh, how can the sinful one profit, ask all commentators. How can the one who has been exposed to sin, who has been corrupt and vulgar against G-d have attained some benefit, have reaped profits from sin? This is almost a contradiction in terms. However, now after man has committed this grave atrocity against G-d he has no longer the perfect shelaymoos, the perfect identification with G-d. Now he can only visualize and understand G-d from contrast, from a distance, from afar, "kee mayrachok niraw aylai ha shem mee merchakim" from a great distance removed, far removed and greatly remote from the wilderness, from the forest, from the mountain. Man can no longer be in the garden. Man can no longer be in the gan Eden. Man is now stripped of perfection. Hawidnaw tovaomaytiv dayan emmes the Gemorah comments; now in this present era, in our times we have good and bad, good and evil mixed and merged. On that day byom hahoo yiye hashem echod ooshemo echod, G-d's name will be one singular. Why only on that day, why not now? Because now, the Rabbis comment, there is a mixture of good and bad, we can only visualize G-d, mayrachok from the ruins of baytar, from the upheaval of the Spanish expulsion, from the uprooting of Chmelnitski's pogroms, from the noxious holocaust. However byomhahoo as in our time we have begun to proceed to that historic era, where Israel now answers in a clarion call that Massada shall no longer fall, that our historic destiny until the modern era of our third commonwealth has been one of moshel beroocho. The Jewish spiritual relationship was one of dyan emmes, passivity, surrender, and we could only escape into the four walls of the bais hamedrish. We had only Torah, we could only build internally, we could only submerge ourselves in an underground where we studied, where we grew. The spark of hope was concealed by the splatter of blood.

These sacrifices are to be officiated by Aaron and his descendants. G-d commands Moses that he should attire Aaron, his brother, in the elegant garments of the High Priest, while he was uniquely designated to perform the function of carrying out the sacrificial duties. Similarly, we find also when Aaron died, G-d tells Moses to clothe Elazer with the special garments of the High Priest. The High Priest is to be a symbol of the people. Therefore the Torah does not command the priest to clothe himself. Aaron could have easily put on the clothes on his own and also Elazer could do likewise. Moses however was delegated to clothe the High Priest, symbolizing the people's choice, marking this gala procession with external glamor and glow. Aaron's unique character is expressed in the external adornment and cherished by the entire congregation of Israel. Vyawtsayts tsis vyigmawl shekaydim. His tree blossomed and his staff had been exposed with a freshness that was unlike that of korach. Aaron's staff blossomed forth with a bloom that everyone would easily recognize and discern. Everyone could readily ascertain the great glow and majestic beauty that was indicative of Aaron's character. For Aaron the Torah records the day of his death, while for Moses we have no recollection of any date. Aaron's character is one of external glamor, therefore the Torah records when he was taken away, when his glow departed from Israel. . . . The character of Moses is concealed. Moses didn't know when his face was shining. Moses was not aware of his external character. The concept of the Torah is "Bhatsnay leches," concealment while the function of officiating for the services of the sacrificial duties must be apparent to all, and everyone must be aware of the greatness, of the glory of G-d.

However, on the day when Aaron was annointed, in his greatest moment of pride and glory, his two sons Nadav and Aveehoo were struck down, as the Torah records, while they were offering a strange and false fire that I, G-d, did not command. Aaron who had experienced the greatest day of his life being annointed before all was exposed with the experience of having such a great misfortune placed before him. He was confronted with a tragedy that was unparalleled. In that Haftorah we read likewise of Oozaw, when he brought the arin, ark of G-d, and placed it upon the wagon, while everyone was rejoicing he was struck don, cut asunder, torn aay from Israel, G-d, as it were, reaped his wrath and took vengeance against Israel. On the day of pride and glory, glamor was turned into dismal darkness, into a cloud of gloom, a shadow of despair. Vyeedom Aaron, Aaron was silent. He did not express any criticism. He did not demonstrate with shouting, with a wail, with a bellowing hail of outcry. We kept quiet. This is the word that G-d has spoken. With my near ones shall I be sanctified and the people shall demonstrate the glory of G-d. The sacrifice of Aaron demonstrates to the people the necessity of conquering their emotions in times of stress, of containing their sensitive feelings in an hour of peril. Aaron provides for the people a mission for all times. The message of Aaron on the day of his great glory, when he had experienced so much greatness and everyone saw, everyone recognized, and everyone visualized the adornment, the splendor, the beauty was not only an external feature of Aaron's great capability. There was another inner greatness, inner glow that the people recognized, that Aaron did not slide back, did not sink into any kind of spiritual decadence, nor did he slide into any pitfalls of moral depravity. Rather he contained his bitter feelings and he conquered the inner persecution, the pain, and anguish that he had experienced. Moses complains to Aaron because he did not eat the sacrifice offered on that day, and Aaron said: "Would that be pleasing in the eyes of G-d?" Moses was angry at Aaron because he did not eat and partake in the food for the sacrifice, and Aaron declares on this day of mourning which he has experienced that he cannot participate in joy, in food, in eating, no he cannot. Aaron recognized that although his mission is to perform on an external basis, he has to demonstrate to the people the glory of Israel and the pride of Jacob. Nevertheless he, Aaron, is compelled to relinquish his duty at a specified and appointed time. He, Aaron, is designated at some time to step aside, to walk away from glamor and from glitter. There comes a time when he cannot partake in the service, where there is another higher call of duty. That's the vayeedom Aaron, the silence, stillness, which speaks louder and pours out for greater than any functional duty that he may perform. Thus the leader who has been chosen to perform duly to administer over the functions of even the highest religious character, the leader who has been delegated by G-d to exercise and instruct and officiate is at times called, and required, and it is demanded of him that he secede, and let go. His pride and glory is expressed when he does not demonstrate any outward sign, any external symbol of glamor and glitter. Rather, the idea of his inward piety, of his inward intellectual growth has to be demonstrated to the people. The people must see the greatness of Aaron in another form, in another manner, in another character. Aaron played his role with unique depth, with unique skill, and with unique ability.

How must Aaron and his kinsman enter into the sanctity of G-d's dwelling place, of his mishkan, of his Tabernacle? How is Aaron to encounter G-d and how must he make his proper supplication, and how is he to offer and sacrifice and officiate in his duties? How is he to be the official who is designated to perform as the functionary leader? How is he to exalt G-d and extend the glamor and glow of G-dliness? Bzos yawvo Aaron el hakodesh. In this manner, in this concrete and definitive expression in this mode of religious worship shall Aaron enter stripped of lustful passion, removing his desire for eating, for sumptuous delight. He cannot enter shesooyay yayin, drunk. Intoxication is forbidden, drunkedness is prohibited. There are also special laws for the High Priest, he is forbidden to exercise illegitimate intercourse, he cannot engage in illicit relations. Moreover there are special detailed laws which are designed to promote his sanctity and provide a stringent code of laws whereby he may be a symbolic champion of discipline, to provide a course, a guiding course of religious principle wherein the people shall take example of his noble character, wherein the people shall be guided to walk in an upright and steadfast manner, that they should not slip nor slide into the pitfalls of the spiritual abyss. They should not digress from the path of righteousness, not to be diverted from the goals that have been presented to them, from the mission that they must perform and the duty that they must exercise to enhance their own cultural and spiritual development, to advance the cause of the sublime spiritual ethic for the entire world civilization. Thus we have two categories of passion that have been expressly prohibited in *Ieviticus*: not eating contaminated food, not taking delight in sumptuous meals of various kinds of animal that are unclean, that are despicable unto G1d, so that man may be free from stooping to the animal within him. Man should extricate himself from the bondage of desire, from the slavery of passion that ambushes him and seeks to ensnare him into the mire and depravity of immorality. Man must sublimate his passion for pride, passion for lust, his anxiety for food, and his greed for power must be transposed and transformed into a sublime religious experience. Only then can we ascend to the pinnacle of kedoshim tiyoo, of aspiring to the platform of sanctity, of elevating oneself to the existential height of the ethical good, to reach the sunim bonum that is inherent in man, not to subdue oneself and to be overcome by the passion and pride of the animal in man. Man has an insatiable quest for passion and greed, and his anxiety for lust and power is immeasurable. Material splendor is his aim and material conquest is his goal. Aale al bomsay av adame lelyon. I shall ascend to the height of the clouds and I shall be equivalent to the most high. Therefore the Torah has laid great stress and placed great emphasis on prohibiting many animals and birds that are unclean, and the Torah has also presented many precepts that prohibit the licentious lust to quell the thirst and passion of man's animal desire. Both these desires are termed toomash. If man eats or if he engages in lustful desire he contaminates his soul, and he defiles his character. He uproots his spiritual spark that is dormant within him, and he shuts off the fire of G-dliness. How can one ascend to the spiritual pinnacle of G-dliness? If one strips himself of that burning animated fire of the material goal, if one divests himself of the inane and mundane preoccupations in lust, in greed, in passions and pride, if one divorces himself from these foods that are unclean, from the illegitimate relationships that he may enter, if one removes the fire of licentious behavior, then he can aspire to the license of kedoshim tiyoo, of kindling another kind of fire, a spiritual fire.

Hee hawolaw al moddaw jik gakaukaw. This is the fire of spiritual ethic, of cultural morality that is demanded of man, that the Torah compels man to exercise if he is to retain his tzelem elohim, the image of G-d. If he is to remain, if he is to survive, if he is to continue then the only path is kedoshim, sanctity, holiness, to extricate and liberate himself from the mundane passions and inane desires that seek to engulf him and submerge him in the stormy sea of servitude, in an ocean of terror, in a river of torment that will overflow the cultural spark and dash any hope of his ever attaining a spiritual existence. Therefore kemaseh mitzraimookenaseh Canaan, in the acts of Egypt and in the acts of Canaan you should not engage. You should not immerse yourself in the atrocities of Egypt, nor shall you become overwhelmed and ensnared in the abominations of Canaan. Rather, you shall seek both the internal and external manner of cleaving unto G-d. Israel is prohibited from engaging in exercising and reconciling its frustrations from Egyptian domination by the overindulgence of food, nor should it become overwhelmed by the glamor, or overpowered by the glitter of Canaan, who seeks to demonstrate by its external pride and external passion that Israel should become immoral and depraved by sinking into the spiritual mire of lust and licentious acts that would only strip it of its divine image, that would only divest it of the spiritual spark that can be the only way for true redemption.

Therefore, there are two kinds of light that illumine the Jew throughout his historic travail, in expressing his historic heritage, in conveying the message of timeless morality, in communicating the mission of the timeless ethic. There is a hee hawolaw almokdaw kolhalailaw. There is a flame wherein man elevates himself unto G-d throughout the entire night, throughout the entire dismal darkness, of the dense frustration of diaspora, the thick black cloud of anguish, agony, strife, and stress. There is a light that shines in the darkness wherein man can excel and advance himself, reaching out for the ray of light that lies beyond the horizon. Then there is another way, where man excels and advances. He enhances the cause of a spiritual existence and promotes the goals of his ethical being. That is byom, when there is material splendor, when society is affluent, when Madison Avenue blossoms with the bloom of secularity. Byom tsavasee, when is Aaron to be annointed? In the day time where everyone can see, where everyone can experience that Aaron has demonstrated that he is a shining example for timeless humanity. Although prosperous, although affluent, he nevertheless is more intent on reaching the sublime spiritual plateau. His eagerness is everflowing, everexuberant, and ever more invigorated to make the idea of G-dliness prevail. We have expressed the idea that there are two categories of desire from which man should abstain, namely, illicit relations and reviling and repugnant foods, that the Torah has explicitly prohibited man to indulge in. The Torah has considered these two acts of desire as repugnant and reviling to man's character. It debases and degrades him, and distorts his proper view of spirituality.

The day of Yom Kippur, that solemn and somber day is to atone and moreover to cleanse man from external debasement and internal demoralization of his character. Yom Kippur seeks to elevate and make man reach the supreme height of cleaving unto G-d. It is a day of complete abstention from physical food and a day of ceasing from indulging in relations, even permitted relations; even marital relations that is allowed during the entire year is considered a violation and a desecration of this holy day. There are two seerim that man brings on Yom Kippur: the classic seerhazazel, which is sent to the desert, and the other soyir lashem stands as it were before G-d on the altar. What do there two seerim symbolize? There are two ways wherein man must realize his deficiency, his ineptitude, where he has failed spiritually, where he has not excelled to his potential, where he has not realized those capabilities that are endowed in his tselem Elohim, in his image of G-d, in that spark that should ignite him in a spiritual way. The kedoosha of every day is intensified and structured in Yom Kippur. This is one day where man extricates himself from the passions and fury of everyday life. He recognizes and begins to discern that there are those obstacles that make him sin, when he is in the midbar alone away from civilization, remote from community, set apart from society in his own private, personalized performance, where he has to express his individuality away from the environment, set apart from the social milieu. He has his own kudshay kidoshim, his own inner life, his own inner being, his own inner structure that he must purify and sanctify. He has his own mission to perform, his own goals, aspirations and cultural desires, spiritual aims to achieve. There is another way wherein man must perform. He must achieve within the structure of social conflict, within the organizational structure of communal activity, that is the soyer lifnay Ha Shem. Man sometimes exploits G-d. The idea of religion is very nice, beautiful and he uses it as a stepping stone to latch upon and to exploit and take advantage of those who are downtrodden and destitute. He uses the spiritual idea as a whipping lash to beat upon these that are way down on the social ladder. He attempts to express his great religiosity and demonstrates his supreme spiritual desire for G-d. He shows off conspicuously about his religious fervor, his zeal for G-d and moreover his compassion for Israel. How many people have transgressed in this way? How many people have committed atrocities against their fellow man? How many people have acted in an inane and mundane manner, using the religious symbol to exploit his fellow man, using G-d as a kardum lachpurbaw, as a spade to shovel, to dig out and uproot man rather than to elevate and to inculcate a feeling of spiritual solidarity within the Jewish community? Thus the solemnity of the Day of Atonement is characterized by a firm spiritual resolution on behalf of every individual to realize that there is some spiritual spark that is to ignite him and uplift him above and beyond the mundane, material mediocrity that swooped sown upon him and seeks to enslave him. Therefore we read Vnislach lchol adas bnay yisroel vlager hgur bsochum kee lchol haam bishgagah—that Almighty G-d shall forgive the entire community of Israel and also to those who sojourn there, the stranger amidst you shall also be equally acquitted and exonerated on this solemn day. We have a parallelism between the community of Israel, the in group, and the stranger who is on the periphery, who is a marginal man in the society of Israel. Nevertheless, the Torah has expressed the will and the desire for equal rights and the protection, the exoneration and defense for the stranger, that there is equal pardon for all, no two classes, no caste system, rather all can be forgiven, all can be acquitted, all can be exonerated, and all can be pardoned on this most solemn supreme day. We have two commandments, "Vawhavta lrayacha kmocha" and concerning the ger it is also written "Vawhavta lo kmocha" you shall love your neighbor as yourself and likewise you shall extend that same hope, that same feeling of admiration and love, that same feeling of benevolence to the stranger. It is extremely striking and very significant that we have been commanded equally to love our neighbor and the stranger simultaneously, with that same love, with that same admiration, with that same enthusiasm that has been expressed in the adherence to a mitzvah, to a commandment and precept. Herein the High Priest is celebrated with the higday khoona with the special garments that the High Priest must robe himself on this High Day. Aaron, when he makes his encounter with Almighty G-d, attires himself in garments of splendor and robes himself in raiment that radiate, that express the luster of G-d, and enhance the shine, the pride and glory of Israel who have been delegated to serve G-d as His faithful and obedient followers. Moses, on the other hand, when he encounters G-d, his confrontation is depicted in very clear and specific terms, "shal na lechaw mayal raglechaw," divest yourself of your shoes, take off your clothes, your garments and strip yourself. The wearing of shoes, as we note in Isaiah, "and he walked barefoot," is indicative of someone who is in strife and stress, in turmoil, and torment, who has lost power and has sunken from pride. Moses, on the other hand, is characterized with the subdued element, with the subordinated characteristic of a servant; when Moses encounters G-d there is no pride and there is no glamour, there is no glory and there is no luster. Moses must perform the mission that he has been delegated to fulfill. He must enact and execute the task that has been delegated to him. Therefore, we recognize a contrast between Moses and Aaron. Moses, the intellectual, creative leader, divested of material splendor and divorced from external glamor, from external glitter. "Kee korah or pawnuv, is required to wear a ofmasue, a mask, because there is a certain partition, a division between Moses and all of Israel, while Aaron is attired in splendor, adorned in the pride and glory of Jacob. "Tzadikkatawmaw yifroch werez balvunun yisge"—There are those righteous men who are assigned with the noble task, with the noble mission of expressing the idea of G-d in a blossoming and blooming environment. They convey the idea of G-d and communicate the entire concept of His law, statutes, precepts, ethics in a blossoming, in a splendorous fashion, in a majestic way. There are others who give expression to G-d in the levunun, in the forest; in the midbar, in the dessert, in the mountain, or on the plain, away, distant, remote, and far removed from the community. They have their own kudshay kodshim, their own inner sanctity, their own four walls where only at times do they convey, contribute in a popular and publicized manner. There are those who wear the kesonas pasim of Joseph, there are those who can only manage to clothe themselves in a meel katan of Samuel, in a small mantle. Some leaders are destined for external glamor, external glow; others are only destined for internal growth, internal development. Some are adorned with splendor and the halo that is attached to a great public figure, who makes his presentation on the stage of public and communal life, who makes his presence felt in the arena of social and societal battleground. There are others who have another mission, another kind of goal, another kind of task; they are directed to the meel katan, to the small mantle, disguised and concealed from the public, communal, and social hub-hub. They are divorced and segregated, isolated and far removed from the mainstream of the majestic and material beauty of activity and participating in the functions of public life.

"You shall not defile or contaminate the land for if so, it will spew you out." The Torah warns Israel that if they contaminate the land and if they pollute the soil with abominations and desecrations of the Law, then they shall not be meritirious of settling on it. They will not be able to inhabit it, nor will they endure on the land that G-d promised to their forefathers. Hence Israel is endowed with a unique and specific sanctity, with a holiness that permeates throughout the very essence of this soil which radiates and permeates with kedoosha, holiness. Its character is above and beyond the average homeland of a nation. It is consecrated by, is hallowed by Almighty G-d. We dare not profane it nor may we defile it, or contaminate it.

There is another yet further, and more durable positive quality of the sanctity of the land of Israel. That is that every Sabbatical year must be observed as a year of disengaging, disassociating and discontinuing all types of agricultural productivity, that man must rest, and cease from labor, from physical arduous toil, plowing. Reaping the soil is abandoned and the land rests unto G-d. The land that man exploits, and tills and reaps its harvest, the land that man conquers, subdues, overwhelms, overpowers with his laborious, tedious work and effort is transformed into a holy and sacred symbol. A sign of spiritual rest is endowed in the land that we may observe the land in a different perspective, in a new view. The national sovereignty of Israel is predicated on a system of sanctity. We are not to inhabit this land as mere creatures of conquering space. We are not to inhabit Israel as men embarked on a geographical conquest. We are not to inhabit Israel and to exploit it by the use of our physical power, military exploits, or tactical and strategic military maneuvers. Rather, Israel is endowed with kedoosha, with an element that is superior to the mere physical status of its limited boundary lines and its geographical location. Israel must observe, therefore, both the negative and positive commandments that insure the sanctity and enhance the hallowed majestic aura that is attached to the land. Its sovereignty is not merely pure nationalism, the pride of a homeland, the power of the human community to grasp hold of land, to seize upon the soil and to capture territory. This is not the mission of Israel, nor the task of Zion, nor the goal of Jacob. The mission of Israel is "kedoshim teeyew," how we may be sacred if we transform and transpose the character of a national sovereignty into a specific and unique holy boundary line, a boundary line that is dedicated to serve G-d with mitzvos, with precepts and commandments of leket, shikchaw, payau—of those tithes that man gives to those who are impoverished or to the Priests who are to serve intellectually and to perform the spiritual goals, heightening and intensifying the communal educational status. This is the service of the soil, to ameliorate the plight of the needy, to advance the cause of intellectual creativity, not to submerge and to bury our cultural mission in a pride of soil. For the blood shall defile the land and whoredom shall desecrate it and it will no longer be able to contain you. We are also commanded to adhere to Israel's soil in a positive way of shemitah, abandonment. Only if we abandon it, cease from physical toil, abandon agricultural exploits and declare unto G-d that the land indeed belongs to Him and we only have a lease of operating it, then we may be able to purify ourselves intellectually and spiritually. This is the function of national sovereignty. It is only a sign for advancing our cultural creativity. It is only a symbol for enhancing our spiritual goals. We are not to be enslaved by the soil, by the feeling, and pulse of conquering power. This is not Israel's funtion. This is not Israel's duty of performance. "Vhaaretz lo seemucher itzmesoos"—The land cannot be sold for an everlasting eternal time, for at yovel the land reverts to its original owner, symbolizing therein that there is a continuity of ownership. That although eretz Israel is sold whether willingly or if it is compelled to be sold, the land shall revert back to its original owners on the appointed time. Vhaaretz ezkor, and I shall remember the covenant of former times, and also I shall remember the covenant with Abraham, Isaac and Jacob, and then the sentence concludes, vhaaretz ezkor, also I shall remember the landuztirtze haaretz es shabso schaw, then the land shall become consoled and appeased from the long desolate waiting time, from the great period of decimation, when the land was not inhabited, when the land was without citizens, without its people. The land itself shall remind, awaken, as it were, G-d to once again remember his covenant with Israel. The land of Israel will be a symbol of the people's continuity. Although we have not meritorious facts of ethical and moral deeds, nevertheless that time will precipitate an era, an age, when the land will be resuscitated to awaken us, that our social consciousness and moral concern will be rekindled by the resettling of Israel. The land itself shall open up its boundaries and expand its frontiers to arouse our ethical spark of human decency, to awaken that burning and animated desire to be concerned, to be aware of our brethren both culturally and socially. The land itself, the land that contributed to the intellectual creativity of the kohain and to the social stability of providing for the anee shall once again open up its boundaries for advancing the cause of human justice.

We have thus far discussed three manifestations of sanctity: sanctity in food, not in indulge in excessive food, in excessive eating and drinking, not in indulge in illicit relations that defile our character, to deny ourselves from immoral sexual gratification; and cessation of agricultural toil on the Sabbatical year. We come to another degree of sanctity that the Torah has required of us. "You should not desecrate My Holy name, so that I may be hallowed and sanctified amidst the children of Israel." The sanctity and sacred hallowing of G-d's holy name is our most duty bound obligation. We read in the Decalogue "you should not profane G-d's name." In *Leviticus* we have an incentive, a new interpretation that we must hallow G-d's name, sanctify it, and convey this holy idea, communicate this divine thought to increase the flame of His faith and to elevate the spark that is dormant within us, the spark of radiating sanctity that permeates when enhances, that vibrates when advanced in a spiritual and intellectual manner.

There is another tookad aish, another kedooshah, another sanctity when man expresses his burning zeal and animated desire to fulfill the obligation and to perform his duty bound commitment of hallowing G-d's name. This fire is the flame of history that calls beyond the everyday duty, that clamors above the daily arduous chores that man undertakes. It is the unique proclamation of our historic heritage that defies all nature and stands above man's mundane material aspirations; it uplifts man from the bondage of material servitude and extricates him and ameliorates his plight of sliding into the pitfall of spiritual abyss, moral decay, and ethical degradation, and depravity of his soul. This is the fire that brought us through the furnaces of many persecutions that were heaped upon us. This is the burnt offering of the many ashes of two millenia of misery, misfortune, agony, aggravation. This is the sum total of our stress and strife that we have endured throughout the two millenia.

"The world stands on two pillars," declares the Tosfos in Bronchos, on "yehay shmay rabaw," al sidra dekedooshta—that we sanctify in nakdeeshocha as the angels sanctify G-d. There are two pillars, the yuchinand the boaz, as it were the strength of containing oneself amidst persecution, of conquering the anguish and not succumbing to the agony of the colossal catastrophe that was culminated in the second World War. Yehay shmay rabaw, let thy great name be hallowed, magnified, sanctified is the cry and outpour of the bitter soul, the distraught heart, and the aggravated person who is perplexed with the dilemma that there is no guidance. "Nisteraw darkee mais

Hashero"—The path is concealed, the road is closed, the avenue is blocked off, there is no sea to navigate in, there is no ocean to journey, there is no river to voyage. All avenues of hope have been terminated. All highways of encouragement have been cut off. We are cut asunder and torn apart from the Holy One, blessed be He. We are severed from the mainstream of the world civilization. We have no yearning for any cultural activity. We have no desire to express any praise, any blessing, any prayer. We are cut off, taken away, and shut off from communication. In this dark despair, in this dense overcast, a voice calls from above and the Holy One speaks from beyond that within the flame and through the ashes shall emerge a more refined, a higher ethical, and more definitive cultural person. This is the voice of ultimate dedication unto G-d during the turmoil of exile and the frustration in being forgotten, and forlorn, forsaken from G-d. There is another way of manifesting and expressing one's devotion and dedication to G-d and that is in the manner of the angels. When there is a complete spiritual blissful relationship from man to G-d, when man reaps his material splendor and is culturally creative eesh tachas gafno and eesh tachas tayainawso, man sits under his fig tree and the fruits of his labor are transformed and molded into cultural creativity, into intellectual productivity. When man can sing out his praise, when man can express his sheerah, his song unto G-d, that there is perfection and harmonious delight, satisfaction gushes forth in a continuum like the angels sing the sweet homage of Almighty G-d. Both universal and particular merge and blend in one harmonious unison, kadosh, badosh, kadosh Ha shem tzvawos malo kol haaretz kvodo and borooch kvod Ha shem mim komo, G-d is sanctified, magnified and hallowed from the universal community and particular community. This is the voice of the angels. These two forms and modes of expressing one's kedooshah and kadish are signally demonstrated in the two sheeros, in the two songs of Moses; Hazinoo and Uz Yusher. The song of the *Exodus* is one of great jubilance over the deliverance from servitude where we reap the fruit of our spiritual harvest, rawasaw shifchaw al hayum. Even the servant, the handmaiden saw at the ocean the great miraculous wonders, was a witness to the great supernatural intervention of Almighty G-d. The song of *Exodus* is characterized by a sense of beauty, a dignity, and majesty. It is one that we perceive with our sight, we empathize it, we experience it, it is our essence, our pride, our glory. It is the abundant, intellectual, and creative flow of Israel's contributing grace to the nations of the world. There is another song that characterizes the essential drive in experiencing the supreme test and awesome travail that encompasses the Jewish nation. When Israel is emerged in the depths of despair then we hear the cry of Hazinoo, of Listen! Harken! Moses' farewell address, his farewell song of Hazinoo is one that renders ethical admonishment. It is a song that expresses the idea that we must adhere to G-d's principles, to G-d's ethical commandments, to these moral precepts throughout endless time, throughout timeless history, throughout the continuum of our unique heritage.

It is a cry and a lament of vayishman yeshoorin vyeevat Israer, yeshoorin, become swollen in pride, fat from material splendor, and its heart was hardened not listening to Almighty G-d. They cleaved no longer to his commandments. They adhered no longer to his precepts, for Israel liked to walk in its own pleasre, engage in its own lustful activities, become immersed in its own greed, envy and power. Therefore Moses declares, "Vayeetosh Sloha awsayhoo." And you forgot the G-d who created you, who formed and shaped you tzur yelodchaw teshee, the force that formed you. These two songs are conveyed in the idea of two motifs in prayer the kadish and the kedooshaw. The kadish represents hazinoo that G-d is magnified and sanctified in time of stress, in an age of strife, in period of turmoil throughout enduring time and we praise G-d although passively and submissively for we cannot be active participants. The kedooshah on the other hand is our expression like angels, our expression of pride, our expression of G-d's glory. Therefore kedooshaw represents tachas kevodo yookood yookol keked aish. Underneath, behind, above and beyond there is concealed a fire of purification. Vetzrof kabor seegayich vaseeraw kol bedeelayich —to purify to melt away the dross, the filthy, ugly, corrosive, and corruptive elements that catch hold and grasp onto the house of Jacob, and fill his tent with abomination. They clutter his home with shameful scorn with mockery, with abuse and misuse, with reviling and repulsive acts of atrocity against G-d and negligence against his fellow man. The tamay tomay yikraw, the one who is polluted with contamination, the one who has defiled his character in toome—from the semantic essence of tum, filled up, overflowing with filth, with disdain against G-d is the one who indulges in excessive food and drink, who indulges in lust and licentious acts engaging in illicit relations. He immerses himself in the physical geographical land abusing it, pillaging and conquering other lands, exceeding his boundary line and becoming subdued to teh soil rather than transforming it to serve him that he may be guided along the road of spiritual service, of spiritual fulfillment. It is the semantic idea that mikueh Ha Shem yisroel—the term for purity is equated and identified with hope. "Kavay el Ha shem chazak vyaamaitz leebechaw." "Leeshoouschaw keeveesee Ha shem," in hope we can find purity. Whatever is, is hope, declares the poet Alexander Pope. Hope is man's salvation that in time of stress he looks upward to the outstretched hand of G-d, of Ataw nosain yadl pashim. Those who have stumbled, those who have neglected their true path poshim yeekoshloo bum kee yesharim darchay Ha shem, those who have lost the true road, who have lost their way on the road toward G-dliness, they can find and look up to the hand of G-d.

The book of *Leviticus* is one that purifies man, it sanctifies man, it elevates him to the spiritual pinnacle of sanctity that is the highest rung on the ethical ladder that one may attempt to ascend. In aspiring for kedooshah we have two motifs, one is characterized in mikueh Ha shem Yishoe, in hope, in longing, in yearning, in seeking, in striving for G-d in kavay in hoping toward a straight line—kav is a line. Man hopes that he may find the right line to reach G-d. "Lawleches bidruchuv" vhodataw them es haderech yailchoo vaw, to know to make known to Israel the path wherein they may walk haleechos olumlo. The paths of the world belong to Him, to Almighty G-d and when one immerses himself in the waters of the mikveh, he expreses the supreme hope, the supreme wish, and desire that he may courageously be able to fulfill G-d's precepts and commandments. Kedooshah however purifies by the experience of endurance, of sacrifice, of burning devotion, fiery dedication on the flame of historic destiny, even if there is no hope. Even if life is burning he nevertheless serves G-d and aspires to fulfill the will of G-d. Thus *Leviticus* begins with the sacrifice of a person's material wealth; of his ship, hisanimanls, his flock, his herd. Then in bechookosai we read of erochin, that is if a person declares that he wants to give his own value, his own personal value to G-d, he declares that he wants to give of himself. This is a higher symbol of dedication, this is a more elevated motif, a more courageous element in sacrificing unto G-d.

The soldiers of G-d begin now to embark on their courageous voyage throughout history. They begin to commence the advent of their historic journey that will take them throughout the millenia of history, and having the ideas of sanctity before them being delivered from Egypt, having the notion of freedom and sanctity as the essential quality of their being their army is in full combat readiness to undertake their spiritual task and their cultural obligations that have been delegated and prescribed to them. Therefore, vhawyaw machanechaw kadosh—your camp should be holy, divorced from all kinds of uncleanness and to divest yourself of all types of contaminations. All ugly abominations should be severed, cut off, and stripped away from your camp. Vaal tzvo and on the front is the degel (flag) of Yehudah. Israel shall now and forever be the standard bearer of the flag of G-d. They shall carry the symbol and bear the torch of the Almighty throughout their historic timeless destiny, throughout their historic cultural heritage, throughout their historic timeless destiny, throughout their historic cultural heritage, throughout their historic creative heroic voyage that will emerge. Thus the soldiers of G-d are semantically identified with their precepts in the word tzvawo (tzeevaw mitzvoks) which can be interpreted as carrying G-d's precepts. These are the soldiers of G-d who communicate his tenets of faith and convey the message of His word, of His holiness throughout timeless history. The holy camp, on route, when it begins its march at times is filled with overconfidence, with their self-assurance. They become smug and self-complacent, self-righteous and self-content, with their wonderous deeds with the great accomplishments that G-d had shown to Israel, with the great wonders when he had interceded on their behalf. So problems arise. The internal structure is challenged when external bliss is afforded. Therefore the Torah has given heed to the woman who has deceived her husband and become a harlot. If a woman has contrived to be unfaithful, if she has plotted to abandon and desert her faithful relationship then she must drink the bitter water in the ensuing script and ceremony that is performed to expose the hidden lustful desire, to expose the deceptive desire, to expose the deceptive dangerous cunning and conniving person who has attempted to debase, defile and contaminate her blissful marital relationship. Thus when the family structure is challenged and the inner home life is in peril then the very fabric of the society is in danger, the communal structure is being proven whether it can withstand the pressure from within. When the society has attained cultural bliss from without it comes to grips with problems, with its inner development, its inner structure and inner growth. How does the society treat the problem of family divisiveness and how does it seek the solution for family problems? There are two ways, two motifs in combatting the problem of social relationship. The one is brought about by the nazir, the one who abstains from wine, from material splendor, from material abundance, from material affluence, and is a solution which leade to a monastic life, divorced from pleasure and divests oneself from the external glamour and halo of the material world. There is however another manner that is the kohain—the one who is involved in creating a society within the problems and within the conflicts that may arise because of material abundance and economic affluence. There is a parshah in the Torah of yivawrechechaw hashem byish morechaw that he blesses the society of which he is an active participant, a dominant force that wheels, that turns, and uplifts rather than seeks to escape and extricate himself. He is not the nazir—who is the elite, selected to run away and seek G-d in the desert, in the wilderness, in the forest, or on the mountain tops. No the kohain acts within the context of human problems, human strife, and he seeks to develop the cultural climate within the society that he lives in. The kohain seeks to preserve, maintain, to guard, and uphold the various structures and functions of society, to build a bridge between man and G-d, to fill the vacuum of material splendor with spiritual bliss. Therefore the Torah has keenly connected the portion of the sotah with the nazir and the kohain to teach us that when problems that tend to divide and disrupt the unity and harmony of the community, then there are two methods to cure, to remedy, and to seek aid for that group. They can seek a refuge in the nazir, the one who abstains from the vine grapes, from all beverages that tend to give the power, the lust, the feeling of domination and dominion, the acts of power, the feeling to pollute, and to make tuma—to contaminate society by vulgar and corruptive acts that corrode and spoil the very essence of the spirit. The nazir abstains from the power of society, from the wanton lustful domination of man. He seeks a refuge—mee yitnainee bamidbar mlon orchim. At one point the prophet cries and laments, who can give me a place where I can divest myself from the main currents of this brutal and corrupt vulgar people. Then instantly the prophet reminds us, it was a fire grasping me and I was inspired, overwhelmed and transformed that I could not divorce myself of the cultural currents and the mainstream of social turmoil and intellectual torment. I could not flee from the frustration of my fellow man. Rather, I had to envelop myself, to become involved in the problems of my people, to immerse myself in the strife and the stress of the nation. Vhawyaw kaish utzoor biatsmosai—the feeling for the nation evolved and expressed in the prophet such an overwhelming and awe-stricken experience that he could not flee from the root and core of the problem. He was rather compelled to seek prayer, to seek a pardon for his nation's iniquities, transgressions, and atrocities which they have committed against G-d. This is the mission of the kohain in yvorechechaw and yishmorechaw of yoair and yeesaw—that there is a solution within and not necessarily to seek refuge and escape from without, to be a part of and not separate from—being an integral working unit of and not to seize only on disintegration, pessimism, and corrosion of the society.

Aaron is commanded with the precept of bhaaloschaw eshanairos—to lift up the candles to illuminate society, to convey the light of G-dliness, and to communicate the incandescent radiance of Almighty G-d to the nations of the world, to the entire civilization el mool pnay hamenorah to the central point. From the center of G-d shall emanate cultural creativity and intellectual productivity. In time of bliss we express to G-d in the voice of the shofar, atekeeaw. In all our sacrificial duties and obligations unsikatem bachatsotsros to blow a tekeeaw. What is the significance within the concept of tkeeaw and trooaw that in time of blissful association, in blissful relationship we blow the tkeeaw, in time of agony and aggravation we blow the trooaw, the symbol of the shofar? This symbol of tkeeaw and trooaw is essential to the outcry, and the quest of our historic message. There is a tkeeaw in Jewish communal life, and there is a trooaw. There is a time for tkeeaw and a time for trooaw. The tkeeaw is described in our literature as a simple straightforward blast, while the trooaw is one that breaks through small waves, either of three or nine, whatever. On Rosh Hashanah we combine them both and express our tkeeaw and trooaw. Moreover on Rosh Hashanah the seder (order) is not only tkeeaw and trooaw but we also conclude with tkeeaw. Thus we begin with tkeeaw, the middle blast of the order is trooaw and we convey the final blast with the tkeeaw. The question is what is the significance of this seder, of this order that has been the tradition on the High Holy Day of Rosh Hashannah? Societies have growth, strength, and power, then they seep into spiritual decay. They fall into the mire and slowly disintegrate until they are completely obliterated from civilized life. They experience growth, great material growth, great abundance of economic affluence and then they begin to decay spiritually and materially until they are completely eroded from the earth. Judaism on the other hand has this resilliance, this rejuvenating factor, this resurrecting ability that we have a continuing historic heritage, that we continue, that we survive, that we maintain, and we are a vibrant dynamic force in the life of society. There is a time for tkeeaw and a time for trooaw, an age for the simple straightforward blast and a period when there s trooaw overwhelming overshadowing perplexity with a dilemma and despair and a problem of peril which is exceedingly great, traumatic, and titanic. These two ages clash and are intertwined. Sometimes there are periods of rest "vtishkothaaretz arbawy m shanah" as we read in *Judges*. The land was quiet, ceased from the stress and strife of constant battle, confrontation and overpowering enslavement by the enemy, with the encounter of cultural strife. There is another period where we find ourselves in an overwhelming perplexity. We cannot even imagine how complex the situation is. It is above and beyond any conceived notion. We are not even involved, we are so removed, we are so distant from the cause of the problem that we cannot even see the solution. It is a period of constant strife, ceaseless turmoil, everlasting torment. It is shever algabi shever one salamity heaped upon another, one catastrophe heaped upon another. This is a trooah, a voice that is broken, splintered and shattered and finally on Rosh Hashanah we end the seder, the order of blasts with a final tkeeaw, that although we endure immense suffering and we observe ceaseless agony, nevertheless we shall retain our spiritual heritage. We shall continue to perform our mission. We shall uphold the everlasting promise that the mission of Judaism is to convey the cultural heritage of our forefathers throughout enduring time. Although there is immense and terrifying trouble insurmountable to the naked eye we shall nevertheless attain to the spiritual plateau and we shall ascend to the summit of sublime religious experience. To wage war, to endure in battle, even to triumph after overwhelming suffering, to survive although we have been stripped of so much pride, so much glory is indeed a feat of great spiritual military strength. To this we send out spies, mraglim to seek and lsoores haaretz to make a tour of the land, to survey the geographical location. Can we survive amidst material abundance, can we attain the spiritual plateau in face of great economic affluence, can we reach out to G-d even there is great wealth, swollen materialism, a vyishman yishboorin and nevertheless adhere to G-d, to his precepts, to his commandments, to advance in material progress and to enhance thereby our spiritual status? This is indeed a very great problem. It is a great task and moreover an exceedingly difficult mission to fulfill. After the mraglim failed in their mission because they said there are great giants, the land is great, gigantic, wc will not be able to conquer it, we cannot ascend, we cannot attain, so we shall experience failure. This was the everlasting failure of the dorfhemidbar, of the generation of the wilderness, the wasteful wilderness, because they were not able to excercise their experience of G-dliness within the context of the material affluence. We will not be able to convey our goals and tenets of high spiritual theology, no hachazak hoo mimenoo. No the land is too complex; we must remain in the wilderness; we can only maintain our identity far away from the mainstream of civilized life. This is the answer of the mraglim, this is the conclusion of those who are not able to see with vision. Only kolaiv ben yefooneh and yehoshooa bin noon are able to see with vision. Further on in the conquest of Canaan, they too send out spies to see the land, to tour and navigate, to see what is doing because they had to follow in the footsteps of Moses. Moses had sent spies but he could not fulfill the promised land, the promise of G-d to Abraham because they (the spies) stumbled on the path and were overwhelmed by the great mighty power and were awe stricken by the tremendous strength and military prowess of Canaan. No, this was not the answer of Joshua. He fulfilled the word of G-d; he was able to continue because he advanced and confronted the enemy on his own terms. He advanced over great and insurmountable odds. He sent spies to survey the land and subdue it on a spiritual, cultural plane. Physical conquest is brought about by this shofar by the blasting of the horn against the city of Jericho. The shofar that represents shifrah, beauty, the beauty of Jacob, the pride of Jacob is brought into the midst of the battleground and to the forefront of the military field of engagement. Moses commands the Jews after they failed in their report, after they were submerged in spiritual failure to wear the tsitsis, to garb themselves in the garment of the fringes. Why? To observe others, to survey others, to experience others one must be able to survey and understand himself, to look himself before he observes others, to prepare oneself in readiness for his own spiritual battle before he is able to convey this confrontation to the civilized world: Tsitsis, henay zeh maytsits min hacharakim—Piercing through your own personal life, examine your own character, and look through to see what are the obstacles in your path, what are the stumbling blocks on the road for spiritual progress? How can you attain the ultimate sublime religious experience? What do the blue and the white, the lavan and the tchaylis symbolize? Lavan is white, straightforward pure. Tchaylis blue, it is colored, to retain a balance between my own straightforward personal life, between my own lavan, my own pure life, my own spiritual heritage and the tchaylis, the color, the one that's adorned and attired in material splendor, the blue, the wonderful, the exotic of nature is the tchaylis, the lavan is white, pure like snow. While the Jews traversed the desert and while they were on their journey to Israel they had encountered many inner strifes, clashes, and conflicts, which almost overreached beyond control and extended beyond cultural and spiritual discipline.

There were two major revolutionary outbreaks that were recorded in the Bible, the insurrection of Eldad and Maydad. Moses tells and decries the situation that he cannot control the Jews alone. Then he gathers unto himself seventy elders, seventy statesmen who are to be the elite in counseling him on matters of policy. Two remain in the camp. They were concealed and isolated in their prophecy and they continued to prophetize. Joshua runs out and cries out to Moses, "lock them up, cast them out, cut them off because they seek rebellion, they endeavor to insurrect against you." Moses with his great humility declares, "Would that it be that the entire Jewish nation should be prophhets, should be able to manifest the Divine spirit and attain to the degree of prophetize." Moses is willing to understand and he has consented to adhere to the demonstration of Eldad and Madad. He is determined to examine their grievances, to learn why they disagree and disapprove of him. He is anxious to examine their claim. He is concerned to learn about their reason for dissent, their arguments for disagreement, for discontent with his policy. This is a spiritual revolution, one designed to expand the cultural creativity of the nation, to enhance the intellectual development of the people, to advance the moral and ethical stature of the nation. This is a machlokis lshem shemayim—a revolution for sake of Heaven, to advance the cause of G-dliness in the world. There was another revolution, one of a different nature. The Jews were filled with discontent over the aristocracy with which Moses, Aaron, and Miriam had aligned themselves. Korach his kinsman and his clan assembled against Moses. They attempted to pour out their wrath against the power structure of the Amramic clan. Why should they be in control? Why should they continue to be an aristocratic elite? Why should they wield all the power and command policy? Why should they be in the forefront of the political arena and everyone should bow down to their wishes, everyone should comply to their edicts? We want our own gdoolay, we want our own greatness, we want to form our own power elite, our own power structure, our own pressure groups, our own aidah wherein we shall be able to exercise control to eliminate the power party of Moses. Why should Aaron be at the helf of the priesthood? Why should Aaron be at the primacy of the external glory of Israel? Contends Korach, let us assume leadership, let us arise and rebel against Moses. Who is Moses that he should maintain this tyrannical and demagogic rule? G-d consumed Korach. The earth swallowed up Korach and his entire group that had assembled to downgrade Moses. No, G-d answered: lo chayn audee Moshe, Moses and his family are the true leaders; Moses and his family are the true aristocracy those who assume responsibility and are concerned, involved preoccupied with the problems, perils and dilemmas of Israel. This is Moses, who did not abandon his people in time of the golden calf, who did not mislead his people in the time when they sinned, when they sent spies and brought back the evil and malicious report against the land of Israel. No this is Moses who prays to G-d even though Israel has committed a grave atrocity in not realizing its mission, in not seeking to exercise and fulfill its heroic, historic destiny. Moses falls on his face and prays, he is filled with compassion, and overwhelmed with sorrow for his people who have sinned. This is the true Shepherd, he does not forsake his sheep when the wolf seek its prey, whether its an external wolf or an internal one. No, Moses when he's confronted with the cultural, intellectual wrongdoings and shortcomings of his nation even though he sees their mistakes, he seeks to heal, to stretch out a helping hand, to assist them when they have fallen. Sulachnoo laavon haam hazeh kee godel chasawdechaw kaasher naw sawsaw laam hazeh mimizrayimvaad haynaw. Forgive this people for their inequity, transgression, and their atrocity that they have committed against you for they have not realized and fulfilled their obligations to their potential and to their capabilities. Korach is a material, revolution, an economic discontent, a rebellion of affluence, a rebellion that seeks greed, power, envy, and lust, to cut down power by exercising and wielding their own power. This is Korach, his ambition is overwhelming, his drive, and capacity, and yearning, and zeal to conquer, to extend himself, to reach out and to grasp hold of Moses is obnoxious, repulsive, and repugnant to Al-Mighty G-d. Therefore G-d swallows him up with all his wealth, material affluence. No Korach, you will not attain your venomous and vile plot, no you cannot subdue Moses. "Moshe avdee, Bchol baysee nemun ho"—He is the true, he is the one who is destined to be that prophet of Israel that no one can even consider or imagine to aspire as being his equal. Moses was even confronted by discontent and disapprovement from within his own immediate family. Aaron and Miriam are angry at his familiar relationship and his marital association with Tzipporah. The Bible does not describe the argument, the dialogue and the disapproval that Aaron and Miriam raise against Moses. Rather, the Bible just declares that Miriam was mitsoras, she had leprosy. The pretty Miriam was stricken with leprosy. The Rabbis contend also that Aaron was likewise stricken with leprosy. Mlamaid shenitstara Aaron. Moses however intercedes on their behalf and expresses his sympathy and understanding for his immediate family. Perhaps they felt that Moses was not sharing his experiences with the family. Moses was too much alone, separate, and above and beyond them. He was not involved with his own family, he was not engaged in their problems. G-d answers, "No bechol baysee nemun hoo." Moses is the true prophet. Perhaps this is why Moses asks Jethro that he should accompany them on the path of the midbar. Why should Moses express his anxiety that Jethro should be a guide in the desert? Surely there were supernatural ways, supernatural occurrences like the pillar of fire that would lead the Jews in their journey through the desert. Rather, the Bible wants to report that Moses did have a rapport with his family, that Moses was able to enhance the glory of his family and to provide for the welfare of his kin. Therefore he was interested that Jethro should accompany him. He was interested to uphold and to maintain his family life with Jethro.

This is the law concerning the red heifer, that if a person dies in the tent, the deceased contaminates all within the tent. All objects that are disclosed, that are not concealed without the tsumid puseel become contaminated and defiled, after which the Torah relates the episode of Miriam's death. Why then is there this connection? What is the relationship between the two portions? Is there an association that we may assume and explore between the commandment of the red heifer and Miriam's departure? Yes, Adam Kee yamoos hohel. When a person is no longer around, when he has departed from the aaretz, from the society that he has created, helped fashion, and help to advance and enhance, when he has departed from the society that he has assisted in performing its mission, in exercising its goals, then the responsibility, the symbol of the red heifer which designates responsibility for the entire community, must be poured upon the entire ohel. All the vessels and utensils must be sprinkled with the ashes, with the awfur maychates. All the pottery and everything must be immersed in the sprinkling of the parah adlomah of the may chatos because we must assume now new responsibility, new dedication, ever invigorating, ever alert, to explore once again, to investigate once more from anew, from a fresh point of view, that there is within society a way to preserve it and to contribute, to improve upon it, to make it better for its citizens, more liveable, more viable, more dynamic. Yes, Miriam was such a heroine. She performed with valor, the true valor of the ayshes chayil. After Moses had sung the song of the Red Sea of the Exodus then Mirian also declared to the women fold, "Let us sing and express our praise to Almighty G-d, sing unto the L-rd, for He is exalted." Miriam characterizes meenushim bohel tvoruch—the women who make society prosper, who make the community the viable force of creativity. She is the one—adamkee yamoos bohel—cultural who has given and extended her prestige to preserve and uphold to uplift and elevate the society. Thus Miriam from the word rum —elevation—is the woman who expresses the hope for reaching the plateau of spiritual excellence, of reaching the summit of the blissful relationship with G-d. Alee bair enoo luh—As the Jews sung at the Exodus, they also sung in the wilderness when the miraculous discovery of water came about, when they come upon water to drink, to quench their thirst in the dry desert of the arid land. Sing unto the well, exalted well, they declared —Bayr chafaroohaw surim—a well that princes dug. Kuroohuh ndeevay am—It was carved out and hewed by the princes of a people. The cultural creativity of a nation is developed and continued by the plowing and digging, by the groping and probing of the princes and the heads of state, chiefs of government who do not seek self-complacency, who do not regard themselves smug in in their self-righteous attitude. These are the true surim, these are the princes of nobility, these are the captains of our nation, these are the soldiers of Judea, the Generals of Zion.

Freedom is designated as chayroot. Semantically however we may identify it with charoot as the Rabbis did—charoos al haloochos—carved out on the tablets. Do not read chayroos, read charoos. Read freedom for indeed freedom begins with carving up one's soul, with a burning and yearning animated zeal; with a flame and passion of study that inspires, the soul, invigorates the body, and rejuvenates mankind. These are the princes of the soul, the officers of human destiny. Chofshee-cheepsos is freedom. Cheepus is digging, searching for the truth, examining oneself, scrutinizing one's own character, one's own personal development, opening up one's own inner chamber, that sacred vestibule that expresses one's character and conveys the shining light for humanity. Bais hahee hachapaises yerooshalayim bnayros. In that time I will search out Jerusalem with the candles. One may associate these candles with what the midrash has discussed in advancing the concept, idea, and notion of samchoonee bawasheeshos, of sheer hosheerim, bishtay ayshos. He has delighted me with the two fires: the fire of my own personal identity, of personal realization and personal fulfillment, retaining my own heritage and simultaneously enhancing the cultural development of the entire civilization, advancing the cause of humanity, providing for the cultural fruition of society, administering the goals of an ethical communal life, and elevating the stature of the moral destiny of mankind. These are the two flames. One flame is represented in nair Elohim nishmas Adam, the other one is nair lraglee. One is demonstrated in an inward, refined, spiritual glow, one's own neshuman, one's own spiritual salvation and religious redemption. This is the nair Elohim of nishmas Adam, of one's own soul searching, soul developing experience. This pertains to my creative goals that I would endeavor to fulfill, that I seek to perform, that I aim to maintain. There is however a goal, a mission, a message for timeless humanity, for continuing civilization, for the dynamic ongoing movement of society. That is the nair iraglee, the lamp unto my feet, the lamp that conveys the light for the entire humanity, that makes the road to G-dliness shine with an incandescent radiance, with a burning zeal and animated desire to advance the cause of G-dliness along the rugged road of obstacles and stumbling blocks that are placed in the path of reaching the spiritual ultimacy of identification with Almighty G-d. These are the two flames that burn within me, these are the two fires that fill my body and soul with a passion for G-d.

Kadom hashogeh heeshaw—Like a woman who is overwhelmed with the ecstasy for experiencing her passionate desire, likewise must one entertain that same feeling toward G-d. Then one has exercised a love of G-d, then one has come to grips with the feeling of love, of shavah, of v'shavta es Hashem Elohechaw. That love was declared by Rabbi Akiva, that he was always filled with anguish, ridden with grief that he could not fulfill that precept of complete love, expressing one's complete admiration for G-d until the day came when he had to experience martyrdom, when he had to incur self-destruction at the hands of the Romans. Then he realized that he was able to fulfill his passion for G-d. His passion was expressed in the fervor and zeal for devoting his life unto G-d.

When the Jews had exercised victorious campaigns against Seechon and Og, the king of Moab set upon the Jewish community and expressed his desire to uproot them from their complacent position as conquerors and champions in battle. Balsk, as we know, asked the counsel of Bilam and sought his advice for supplanting the Jewish self-confidence. He asked Bilam to go and distort, to dissuade them from the path of uprightness, to go and lead them astray, mislead them, and misguide them. This was the plan and plot of Balak in seeking advice to lure the Jews and to overwhelm them. He saw that Seechon and Og had tried to conquer Jewry by force, by a battle, by strategy in war. This Balak observed was not the way, was not the method to wage battle against Israel. No, he thought of a more intellectual way. He had assumed a new strategy, one that is primarily an intellectual one; to seduce the Jewish community, to induce them into a feeling of confidence, to sneak upon them when they least expect it. *Lchaw awraw l'Yaakov*—We would suggest another kind of interpretation. Go and stir up Israel, arouse the desire of Jacob, wake up their passion, and make them aware of the majestic beauty, of the material splendor of Moab, of its women, to seduce them into the passion of lust, to arouse them into the licentious atmosphere of Moab and its daughters. Israel was now confronted by a new obstacle, a new mischievous plot to deny its destiny and to denigrate its mission to deceive them on the way of gaining a religious goal on the road of reaching for the religious plateau. Moab advances her beauty and exposes her wanton eyes to lure and seduce, to deceive and deprecate the Jewish ideal the zeal of Zion. This is a new kind of confrontation, one that seeks to strip Israel of its cultural creativity by immersing them in the way of the nation, to stir up their passion, and to create a fury for the fire of their emotions. This is the plot of Moab, not to exterminate of annihilate Israel by force. No, they cannot. They are not interested in overpowering them at the military battlefront. No, they are interested in conquering its spirit, its internal growth, its internal development. This is the idea of Moab. With ruthless cunning they try to uproot the fruit of Zion, the fruitful creativity of Zion. This is the plot of Bilam. *Ma tovoo chawlechaw Yaakov*. This is the desire of Balak, to expose the Jew from his contended tents of religious fervor. How beautiful are thy tents!

Why should you be an *am lvadud yishkon,* a nation that dwells alone, separate, and apart from the world community? Come and let us fraternize together. Soon after Israel was momentarily induced by the lust of Moab, by the passion of the Midianites. After one has assumed military conquest he begins to attire himself in pride, to adorn himself in the fury of his great might. We observe this with regard to Dinah, vtatsay Dianh liros bivnos haaretz. After Jacob has successfully conquered Esau then the Bible immediately detours into the episode of Dinah being seduced because she went out to see the pride of the nations. She became infatuated and enamoured with the beauty, with the external glitter and glow of Shechem. Then there is a new awakening, a resounding reverberating quest for G-d expressed in Pinchas ben Elazar, ben Aaron ha kohain who subsided my wrath when I though to consume the children of Israel. When I considered to doom Israel then arose Pinchas who slew Zimri and cut off Kawzbee from diverting Israel from its path toward spiritual progress. Pinchas is the one who defends the character of Israel, who protects the pride of Zion, and who is the zealot for the glory of Israel. Pinchas is the one who is therefore assured of a brith kehoonas olam—a covenant of aristocracy for timeless history, for he was concerned and involved in the continuity of Israel, of its cultural creativity: that it should not be uprooted and diverted from the path of attaining the spiritual plateau. This everlasting covenant that G-d has made with Pinchas is a spiritual bequest, a spiritual heritage. There is however the covenant of physical territory—geographical location that G-d has set aside for his people that they may inherit in their conquest of Canaan. The land should be proportionally divided—the larger tribe should receive a larger portion, the smaller one a smaller portion. Then the daughters of Tseluvchud the son of Chaifeh come nigh unto Moses and declared, "We don't have any portion in the land for our father died and he left no issue but us. Why should we be cut off, cut asunder from the territorial inheritance? Why should we be struck out from the geographical and land accession of Israel? Should we be cut asunder, should we be severed from the bond of the boundary line of Israel? Moses was unable to answer them so he brought their plea before G-d. Thus G-d answers that the daughters of

Tseluvchud speak correctly. They have a legitimate legal claim. They have a right that is duly shared by them. They have a portion in the land and they should obtain a parcel according to the delegated measure allotted to each tribe, to each family. Then the daughters of Tseluvchud have a share in the continuity of Israel. The women have a proper claim, a legitimate argument to inherit their father's land. Here we experience the right of the woman to exercise legitimate property rights, to uphold her economic equality and to maintain a certain material affluece. The woman is not cast aside, she has definite rights. She must also participate in the continuity—historic, and economic, and also philosophical. Miriam sung the song at the Red Sea. This is their historic claim—Af bhain hawyoo boso hanais—They were also involved in the great miraculous intervention that G-d exercised to alleviate his people from the yoke of bondage. The daughters of Tseluvchud have a share in the economic affluence of Israel, in the geographical boundaries, in the very land, the essence of its conquest. Woman have share in prayer. Women have exercised their right of declaring and beseeching unto G-d, declaring their trouble in all times, and proclaiming the song of victory for timeless humanity. Deborah sings the song of heroic conquest. Chana, on the other hand prays on behalf of her deliverance that G-d enabled her to bear children, to give birth. That is the song of Chana, her prayer. She poured our her wrath before Ili and then expressed her supplications unto G-d in an exalted and elevated manner. This is Chana and Deborah. Chana expresses her song unto G-d on the individual level, for her own personal problems that arose in her particular environment. Deborah sings the song for the entire Jewish community on their heroic exploits on the military battlefield. Both women have an equal share in expressing the joy and glee of G-d's miraculous assistance and his benevolent kindness which he has bestowed upon the individual and the community.

The journey of Israel, the voyage of Jacob throughout its historical destiny and unique heritage conveys to the nations of the world that G-d not only dwells where one's domicile can be found, he also is wherever a person travels. Beshuch bechaw cov koomechaw oovlechtchaw baderech—In all your endeavors, in all your daily activities G-d is with you. As it was when the arin, when the ark of the L-rd was moving, Moses declares, "Arise Oh G-d, let your enemies disperse and disintegrate that they should no longer collaborate in their continued criminal activity and behavior. G-d is not only when a person is in his resting place. He is in all man's routes." Thus Rachel who stole the terufim as a symbol declaring unto Lavan that the god of travel, or the symbol of Lavan's success in travel was no longer with him. Also when Michal placed the terafim on David's pillow it was to signify that David was not in his ay. He was not traveling for the terafim were in the house. On the threshold of the Phillistine temple lay Dagan spread out, beaten down by the ark of G-d. The ark of G-d marches triumphantly and all the gods of the nations cannot overcome or overwhelm Him before his path. No one can block His path. No obstacle can be placed before it, and Ezra prays to G-d that on his voyage to Israel he should not encounter any foreign marauders, any pillagers, bands of robbers who lie in ambush to make prey of the defenseless Judeans. Ezra declares, "How can I ask the King for troops lest he say that the G-d of Israel is powerless on route. This is the message of Israel, that in all our travels G-d is with us, Hom kee ailech bigai tzalmuves lo eeraw raw kee ataw eemawdee"—sings the pastoral hymn. G-d is my Shepherd and I shall not want. In all man's walkings in the great journey of life, throughout the intrepid navigation of everyone's stormy sea there is continuity, there is a thread that runs through and grasps man from the shadow of darkness to walk in the image of G-d, that catches hold and grips him from sliding into the pitfall of spiritual plight. It uplifts him and exalts him to the spiritual plateau and the summit of realizing the sublime religious experience.

Thus in traveling or seeking refuge the route is open even to one who slain someone without premeditation, without kavanah—intent to slay. The swree miklut, cities of refuge have been sanctioned to the one who slays without malice. There he can flee and remain in safety until the law shall be clarified. No blood relative of the slain individual is permitted to take vengeance in those cities of refuge. Thus even the slayer is granted a salvation, a home of redemption, a place to rest.

DEUTERONOMY

Chapter 4

Moses is not able to enter into the promised land that G-d has bequeathed to our forefathers and to Israel for perpetuity. David cannot build the Temple although he requests of G-d to build a dwelling place wherein people shall come to adorn with splendor, and admire the beauty of G-d's glory.

Although we find Moses asking and almost demanding of G-d, for G-d said to him to do not increase—al tosefdabayr ayhi of baduvor ha zeh—do not entreat anymore, do not speak to me about the subject, do not converse with me about this. You cannot enter, you cannot come in beyond the River Jordan. And David likewise cannot build a Temple. Moses and David, the architects of intellect and the builders of the nation, Moses who represents toras Moshe avdee, David who is the delegate of mizmor sheer chanookas habay's l'Dovid—cannot fulfill, cannot come into the house, cannot enter into the land, are removed from complete fulfillment. The question is why? What is lacking in the quality of Moses, what is deficient in the character of David that will not allow them to come in, to enter the holy land, to march in to this Temple that they may rightly do what they have set out, that they may truly perform the mission for which they have invested so much strength, so much courage, so much time and struggle. What is the key factor that restricts and restrains them from realizing fully the potential that they have started, invested? The answer perhaps lay in the fact that a man however great must realize that he is fallible, that he is subject to failure, that he cannot attain perfection, that he cannot aspire to the complee total potential. There is always a degree of imperfection that man will not correct. There is always this element that man will not and he cannot fulfill, he cannot reach perfection. This is his limitation, this is his finite quality that he must realize in all his ambitions, in all his aims that he seeks to dominate and yield power however religious the motif is, however moral and ethical the desire is. He must realize that there is something within him that says restrict yourself, remove yourself, you cannot fathom the infathomable, you cannot understand the secrets of G-d, the unknowable. "Hayawdataw," declares G-d unto Job, Moses, the leader, the man who was shouldered with the responsibility and burdened with the yoke to extricate the Jews from bondage, the man who was delegated with the authority to lead the Jews from the desert, the General who laid the groundwork against Seechon and Og, who destroyed tyrants, military dictators, strategists at the battlefield, Moses was cut down from his power. Shal naalechaw mayal raglechaw—Remove your shoes, you cannot wield power in front of me. No. you are a mere mortal, you will not enter into the Holy land, you cannot reside there. No, your domicile is not there, you have fulfilled up to a certain point and there is limitation. One more battle G-d declares to Moses and that's all—finis-achar tayawsayf el amechaw—Then you'll be gathered in, you cannot exercise all your power, all your dominion. There's a measure and degree that is reserved for G-d. David, the warrior, who battled Goliath, the one who went out against the Phillistines, who confronted them and routed them was the superb General, the archetype of the mighty soldier, the one who characterized the majestic power and energetic heroic battleground leader and military strategist, was cut down from building, from the construction, from erecting a sanctuary, a Holy Temple because there is limitation within David just as within Moses. Every man must experience a certain degree of failure for he cannot maintain this feeling of power, this grasp of greatness. Joseph who was the ruler—the shaleet of Mitzrayim—the overseer in Egypt, also had to experience this idea, that power, complete power can only be reserved for G-d. Joseph when he dreams about his brethren and even his father bowing down to him (so interpreted by the rabbis) brings his dreams to his brethren and his father. He asks them about his unintelligible thoughts in time of slumber. Why did Joseph express his desire that they should understand, and interpret and unravel his dream? After all, Joseph was the poser chalum—the great interpreter for Pharaoh. Joseph was able to understand the contrast between the dreams of the sar hamashkim and those of the sar haofim—the toastmaster and the baker. Why does he present his dreams to his brethren? What is the quest of Joseph? What is his desire? What is his intent? There is something that overwhelms him, something, another element that expresses a bewildering position, that impels him to almost ask why he was experiencing such thoughts, why was he delegated with such notions. Because Joseph must have realized that he wants to relinquish power, hi's not concerned with dominion, he wants to remove himself from exercising control. It is not his aim to rule, it is not his desire to conquer, it is not his quest to dominate. However Pharaoh, who is the ruler, is overwhelmed and perplexed, is confronted with an insurmountable challenge that the smaller, the infiinitesimal swallows up, and uproots, and overpowers the fat, the material splendor. Pharaoh cannot understand such a dream and he exposes it to Joseph because Pharaoh has to confide that he is confounded by this situation. Joseph therefore who is able to discern the concept of power is able to ingeniously interpret the dream of Pharaoh. The dream of power, of conquest is no mystery for Joseph. When Jacob dreamed of the solum mootsuv arzah—a ladder erected up to the heaven he does not confide in anyone, he does not express the wish to know what is the symbol of the ladder at this elevation point because he realized and he was cognizant of the fact that the solum, this swinging spiraling ladder ascends only to a spiritual plateau. It is a summit that one must reach from the earth upward, look upward to what is above you, to the spiritual, to the uplifting one, that is G-d. Therefore Jacob need not reveal the dream because it is one of spiritual conquest, not of physical expansion, not of a material gain. No earthly exploits are envisaged by Jacob. He rather visualized a battle against those forces that repel and repulse man from ascending up the ladder. Therefore these are the travels of Israel. The journey is to swing up the ladder to climb above conflict and to leap above challenge.

These are the words that Moses addressed to the entire community of Israel. The Torah is that symbol of wisdom which is the most significant element in the Jewish contribution to the entire world civilization. The Torah is the message of ethical precepts and the mission of the moral conduct to all the nations. They will say and declare, only such an intelligent and understanding nation who has such a great Torah, such great principles endowed in its beliefs, such great moral lessons in its code, is a nation of high intellect and moral integrity, is a people of G-d. Hodoo la shem kiroo v shmo—praise unto the L-rd, call unto His name, vamim aleelosuv. Make known to the nations, His great attributes, and great wonders and miraculous deeds. There is the idea implicit within this verse of the Jewish mission for the world. Not to be isolated in the ivory tower of spiritual development, not to be segregated in the desert wilderness, the mountain region tops, high places, high points away from the center and mainstream of social involvement. Rather the idea of Judaism is to declare the word of G-d, make known the concept of morality. Also the nations of the world will declare, "Bais yaakov lchoo unaylchah. Let us go and ascend to the House of Jacob, to walk in the light of G-d so that our path towards spiritual progress may become illuminated, that we may have a more improved, vibrant living, that we may endure within the context of the social religious ethics of Jacob. Both the active communication from the nations unto G-d and the passive understanding by the nations of G-d is the very core and the central point of the Jewish mission. We do not have a mission of conquest, of military exploits, military prowess. No, this is not our aim nor our goal. We don't desire great territorial expansion nor is our goal and motif to overwhelm and subdue the world. We only entered into Canaan to redeem the sovereign right that we had. Battles in Canaan were only of short duration. Israel was only restricted to a specific designated geographical location. This is your border as it is described in many places and we are confined along certain geographical boundary lines not to exceed our ability in conquest on the battleplains. Other nations have conquered lands as Deuteronomy begins to describe the various nations who are conquered and subdued. However we have to conquer the spirit, to control man's drive, his unquenchable thirst for lust and power, his insurmountable quest to reach and grasp and devour and uproot everything that comes before his path. Our mission is to enrich the nations of the world with the glory of G-d, to advance his precepts and enhance His glory.

Thus King Josiah who had made great reform in abolishing idol worshippers and idolatry during the Frst Temple sees his kingdom split up before him and he dies in battle. The question is apparent, why King Josiah who had instituted so many great reforms, who had aroused the nation to a new ethical peak and awakened them in their awareness toward G-d, why did he fail in battle? Why did he encounter Paroncho on the battle plain? Perhaps it is to teach an emphatic lesson that the explicit mission of Jewish monarchy is only spiritual sovereignty, that as long as Paroncho recognized Israel as a sovereign state it was Josiah's duty to refrain from engaging him on the military battleground. Paroncho only wanted to use Israel as a roadway. Therefore Josiah should have envisioned Israel as merely a spiritual sovereignty, a gateway to the intellectual development of the nations. Therefore the reason why Hezekiah defeated Sanachayriv was that he did not wage battle against him, rather the angel subdued the legions of Sanachayriv. This is to convey the message that once the sovereign spiritual destiny of Israel is established then we no longer must entertain any notion of physical and territorial conquest of geographical expansion. "Lobchayilvlo bkoach kee im beroochee," not with might, nor with power, said the L-rd, of hosts. G-d does not require great physical exploits, His desire is for spiritual development, intellectual, attainment. Therefore, says the Deuteronomist—ayle hadvorim—these are the words of Moses, this is the motif of the Fifth Book, that the plains of war, the grounds of the military battlefield are only transient and temporary scenes. This is not the goal, this is not the aim of Israel.

Esau was blessed with al charbechaw tichye. You shall rule

by the sword, conquer, be a military general, be great and endure on the battleground. That was his mission. The mission of Israel is intellectual creativity, advancing new concepts. The milchamah of Israel is one of groping with the problems of law. The war of Torah is the saying of the Sages. Even if we have to momentarily depart from the law to fight many battles, to engage in military activities, this is only an immediate necessity, it is not the perpetuating principal of Israel.

What then are the pleas of Moses who asks and prays unto G-d, "Why can't I enter into the Holy Land that you, G-d, have promised to our forefathers?" G-d answers Moses, "Do not continue to pray." G-d declares that Moses should stop praying about his inability to enter, to walk into the Holy Land. All that Moses requested qas ebranawvere—let me just traverse the land and see the great goodness of this Holy Land. Why was Moses concerned to let us know that he prayed to enter into the Holy Land? What is so necessary for Moses to confess his concern, to admit his failure in prayer? What is the aim and purpose of Moses in acknowledging his defeat? Moses who was destined to be the adon haneveeim, the master of prophets, the spiritual hero of timeless Judaism declares that although I was successful, lucky and G-d had always granted my request I was at his beckon call and He would answer me; Moshe ydabair vElohim yane noo vkol—Moses would speak and G-d would answer. G-d never concealed Himself from Moses, G-d was never removed, and G-d was never hidden. It was very easy and a simple matter of course for Moses to declare his wish and it would be simultaneously granted. Moses had immediate fulfillment of his ishes. No, however, when we come to the climax of his leadership, we observe that although Moses is great on behalf of Israel, he can redeem them from doom, he can save them from the abyss, from sliding into the pitfall of spiritual decadence and moral depravity, Moses who prayed on behalf of Israel when they sinned with the Golden Calf, when they failed to report about Israel in the proper light was able to beseech G-d and G-d answers, "Solachtee kidvorechaw—I have forgiven them because of your words, because of your prayer, and because of your outpouring of pity for Israel. Moses could also pray on behalf of Miriam, his sister and his own immediate family. He could exercise his power of greatness for he was the man who was called by G-d, delegated by Him to serve Israel on all levels. The mission of Moses terminates at the crossing of Israel. Every man has his purpose to exercise in life. "Al toseef," G-d asks Moses and reprimands him not to continue in his prayer. His timeless quality lies in the fact that he will be gathered up to his fathers, that in his greatness there is failure. This is the outstanding character of grandeur and majesty that we must infer and derive from the great leader, from the master of prophesy, the military general who led the Jews through wilderness and desolation for forty years. Greatness is therefore expressed in the ability to realize and recognize that one is destined to failure, that no one can infinitely fulfill his potential. There is bound to be obstacles and obstructions along the course of progress, and Moses who had probably been convinced of his invincible expression of prayer, of his intellectual capabilities and military prowess was overwhelmed at his inability to ask and plea unto G-d to merely traverse the land.

After Moses is cut off from his privileges, denied from entering Israel he declares to Israel that the nation will indeed inherit a promised land, a land that is gifted by the grace of G-d with material splendor, with no scarcity of food, a land that is filled with the surplus of agricultural products, mineral resources, with all the natural resources that a country needs for its development, its growth, and maturation. The land of Israel therefore is endowed with a special unique qualification, that it can provide for its inhabitants with good and plenty, with much abundance that would be able to insure its inhabitants of a fruitful and productive life one of eesh tachas hafnoo, eesh tachas taynaso—a man could sit under his fig tree and enjoy his vineyard reclining with ease and no one shall disturb him, no one shall discomfort and disrupt his creative worship to G-d, a land that is filled with richness of milk and honey, Moses declares, "You'll come to a land that is filled with houses that you have not built, rich with vineyards that you have not planted so that you may reap with pleasure G-d's grace that he has bestowed upon you. After you have eaten sumptuously and enjoyed the good and plenty of the land, you must bless G-d. Thank Him for the magnificent material abundance which He has given you. Express your admiration and gratitude to G-d for the wonderful life with which He has enriched you and which you are able to appreciate." Why does the Torah not require in specific terms a blessing before the meal, before one sits down to eat? Rather after you have eaten. The Torah expressly stated, "You shall eat and be satiated and then bless G-d for the great goodness that he has bestowed upon you." Why after the meal and not before does the Torah explicitly declare that a blessing is required? When man is hungry and he sits down to eat, he only eats out of his animalistic desires, his natural inclination to eat and devour the food with his animalistic tendency, to sit down at a meal and to quench his thirst with the passion of his pursuit for pleasure. He does not consider any spiritual or creative need when he sits and eats. He is too much preoccupied and involved with the fact that he must satiate his drive, his appetite, and his desire to satisfy his basic needs, his biological drives. Therefore the Torah does not state explicitly for one to bless before the meal as it would only fulfill a negative aspect in man's relationship to G-d. As the Rabbis have amply discussed it is obvious that when a person is hungry he reaches out and extends himself to G-d with a brocha-blessing. However, when a man has already finished his meal, when he has been completely satisfied and he concludes his food and drink, then he is filled with power, he is immersed with greed, and overwhelmed with a sense of boundless power, infinite pride, and limitless selfish desire. He's filled with the ambition to conquer, with a drive to extend his dominion over all. When man is filled with the idea of conquering, and he has satisfied himself, he's not in any spiritual need. Then the Torah required him to make a blessing. The Torah then explicitly stated that you should give thanks and offer your appreciation to G-d. The term brochah is semantically equivalent to grafting lhavrich. Blessing G-d grafts man to G-d. It sews a unique bond that cannot be severed, it ties man with an umbilical cord to G-d. Therefore the Torah remarks aptly concerning Esau that he finished his meal, he completed his dinner and then he despised the bchorah, at the right of primacy in birth, because primacy presupposes a sense of responsibility, a feeling of duty, and a need for obligation. This was despised by Esau. He deprecated and disapproved of spiritual obligations, cultural imperatives were not to his liking. Therefore the Rabbis have devoted much lengthy discussion to the idea of blessing and offering thanks for every kind of food, what ever it may be, whatever it contains.

Verily, Thou art the G-d who is concealed in contradiction, and wrapped in paradox, clothed in mystery, attired in a sense of awe, great wonder. No one can understand the mysteries of G-d, no one can conceive of the problems and perils, the dilemmas that confront and challenge man. Why does man have to encounter so much strife and stress in his everyday activity, in his daily participation in life, in the communal movement of society. Why does man have to suffer and what is the reason for his anguish and what is the explanation of his agony? No one can resolve it. It is above and beyond man's comprehension, far removed and distantly remote from his knowledge. He cannot ever understand or perceive it. Therefore poverty, one of the greatest afflictions of mankind is treated with an enormous vigor and tremendous vigilance in the Torah. The Torah constantly reminds us of our duty and responsibility toward the indigent and destitute of society. The Torah is one guard to protect and defend, to preserve and maintain the rights of the poor. Therefore, he who has been enslaved or cannot find means of economic livelihood must be provided for with funds by the community. Moreover, society must establish the proper means and necessary modes of employment, whereby they would demonstrate the necessary concern and the right cooperation where the poor and enslaved can be redeemed from their poverty and extricated from their plight of dependence on society. Poverty, therefore must be eradicated. We cannot stand by blindly to the fact that people suffer from economic want. "If you have been blessed with material plenty, with great affluence," declares the Torah, "You cannot be smug and self-righteous and content with the fact that you have blessed G-d, that you have offered your religious sacrifice unto G-d. You cannot dispense your obligation by exclaiming unto G-d that I have blessed you, I am a self-righteous person, a man filled with high moral dignity toward G-d expressing my extreme fervor and deep desire to cleave unto G-d." Cleaving unto G-d must be bridged by the gap of caring and feeling for the one who is stricken in poverty, who is afflicted with unemployment. You cannot satisfy your religious quest by merely blessing G-d, for He has provided you with great splendor, material affluence, and economic abundance. This is not the way nor is it the method of religious identification with G-d. What is the way to express your wealth and convey your material affluence? Only in a manner that will alleviate the poor from the bondage of dependance. You have to make available to those who are destitute the proper method wherein they will be able to become participant members and active constituents in society. "The poor are not to be exploited nor can you trample upon the downtrodden, for if you persecute and embarrass the impoverished," declares G-d, "I shall reap my anger and cast my vengeance upon you." Society therefore is the expression of interaction between rich and poor. The rich are not to close their hands and point with disgust or express their greatness and status. Rather they have to extend a helping hand, one that will uplift and enhance the character and insure that the poor person has a right to strip himself from the plight of his anguish. The poor therefore is a person that is on a par with you in society, he is on an equal level. Lo seesaw pnaydul vlo sehedar dul hereevo, when a poor indigent or destitute man comes with a rich man to a legal suit, to a litigation process, you should not serve him with privilege. You should not exact an unjust claim from the rich person. No, this is not the attitude of the Torah. Btsedek tishpot ameesechaw. Rather with just and proper action should you execute justice toward your fellow man. You're not to experience a sense of mercy and pity. No, you have to exercise a feeling of compassion and concern that he might also walk with you in the gate, in the public thoroughfare amidst you. Don't oppress my people in the gate, in sight of public opinion. Do not look down at the poor person when you are in a public meeting place. When you are in the spotlight of communal action do not trample upon the poor, do not exploit him. No, you must exercise, you must transcend your sense of power, your feeling of ambition, your dream of drive to conquer and control by making the one who is on a lower rung, walk and step up on the ladder. Judges and guardians shall you designate and appoint to preserve the statutes of G-d, that you may be able to insure the safety and tranquility of the people. The judge therefore, must adjudicate between rich and poor between the ameeso and between the eesh.

The legislator, the jurist must be able to discern and utilize keen judgment in ascertaining the proper execution of the law, whether it is for a simple man in the lower rungs of society, a plain eesh, one who has not ascended on any particular ladder or status, one who has not made any mark in society, he has no esteem for the one who is the ameeso, his classmate, his colleague, the one who has established himself properly, who has attained spiritual and eronomic wealth. Both must receive equal judgment. Both classes must be observed and listened to with the equal perception and keen understanding of the legislator. The judgment will help to preserve, maintain, and safeguard the stability of the community and the well-being of the society.

If a false prophet should arise to seduce with impassionate pleas or to induce with miraculous signs of superior intervention, we should not adhere to these symbols that seek to ensnare us. We should not become overwhelmed or overpowered by outside external personalities that are engaged in destroying the Jewish community, in severing the Jewish spiritual sovereignty. We have to assert our vigilance and dedicate our zeal toward uprooting and extricating these growths that tend to supplant the Jewish community. We have to eradicate and exterminate these infectious diseases that arise every generation within our own community, within our own group. We must stamp out those who seek to trample upon the Jewish community. We must annihilate those who are plotting to erase the Jewish mission. Therefore ooveeartaw hawraw meekeeberchaw—exterminate the evil, wicked, presumptuous person who arises with malice toward the Jewish mission, with hatred towards our historic heroic message. Such persons must be confronted with a challenge and combated with vigorous fortitude, that we may be able to vanquish them and not be subdued in the ceaseless struggle of maintaining and conveying our unique set of ideas to the world. Marsayich oomachovayich memayeh ydytsayoo declares the nuvee—prophet. Your harassers and anguishers shall arise from within you. From amidst your community shall arise those who seek to obliterate and to ertinguish the Jewish identity. Therefore, with courage we must establish the Jewish heritage, with conviction we must advance the Jewish mission on the battlefront of humanity, on the battleground of civilization. The judge therefore must be a chacham and a peekayach, erudite in law, in the jurisprudence system and have a keen and intimate knowledge of the psychic drives of social forces and social phases of each individual. He must be aware of the social stresses and simultaneously have compassion for his fellow man. He must not exceed the boundaries of his legal knowledge, he cannot overreach this power of his mental capacity. For if so he will slack and destroy more than build and construct. Therefore, the judge is a partner with Almighty G-d in the covenant of creation, in maintaining the security and advancing and developing a future society, one that would be predicated on law, based on justice, determined by an order, that is a peace for all mankind. Thus the bais hamikdush wherein the judges, the sanhedrin sat was not to be carved or hewed from stones that were chiselled with iron utensils, with iron instruments. Because peace is the sine qua non of the Sanctuary of G-d and there within this framework the Sanhedrin sat, against this background the sanhedrin legislated. Within the context of peace we can establish a law. A vibrant law must be mirrored by a harmonious and fruitful life.

The term compromise in the adjudication and litigation process, is called pshawraw. Pshawraw symbolizes the idea that law must be interpreted on an equal level to both parties. We are commanded to settle the case in a manner that will be mutually satisfactory to both parties. Therefore pshawraw is semantically identified with pesher-interpretation. The interpretation of the law is just and ethical if both parties can arrive at a mutual agreement, if both plaintiff and defendant can agree and remain respectful to one another after the case has been decided, after the court has rendered its decision. Then the process of din, of litigation is expressed in the term shootuf lhakodesh burchoo—of taking part in the covenant of creation. The law is that vital tool, that instrument of beauty that expresses man's wish, man's supreme wish and most elevated and noble concern of fulfilling one's obligation and expressing his religious fervor toward G-d. This instrument is the vital force in making, in developing a fruitful and productive society. It is the operating guidepost that gives strength and character to the commercial welfare of a people and to the individual needs of a nation. Only if a nation has a law that is rooted and just in humane causes does it strive toward a government that operates for the people. The government of a nation is developed and structured by its system of law. If there is a jurisprudence code that is a vital force toward molding the community then the government will survive and contribute toward the growth of the entire world community. Therefore the Torah precedes the commandment of delegating judges and assigning statesmen to adjudicate in the court, to make a legal process that shall be the basis and foundation toward the appointment of a melech, of a king. Somtawseem awlechaw melech—you shall anoint and appoint a king over Israel only after you have worked out carefully and planned with great scrutiny a system of law that shall provide for the assurance of leading toward the road of G-dliness. A king who goes out in battle, who wages war against the enemy must carry a scroll when he goes out and when he returns. The king must always be preoccupied with the notion that his government is predicated on the just and noble principles and precepts of law. Only then can he be successful in battle against his enemies. Then they shall realize that his battles are not merely with the pure ambition of conquering, with the limited finite drive for expanding the country's boundaries and geographical location. No, when a king is armed with the Law, with the Ark of G-d, when he ascends on the battlefield then his battles are rooted in a mission to convey to the nations of the world that his contribution is one of ethical and moral standards. "For we have heard," declared the Aramaians, "Kee malchay yisroel malchay chesed haymaw." The kings of Israel are kings that bestow kindliness and extend their grace on the nations of the world. Hence we have a law concerning the "yeefas tor." When a soldier captures a beautiful girl in battle while pursuing the enemy, conquering a female of that nation then he shall not express his desire for lust in a degrading and debasing manner. No, he must take her into his house so that she may undergo a period of debasing her external glamor. She shall take off or remove her beauty by cutting her nails and stripping her hair from her body. This is the idea within the context of capturing a beautiful girl while at war. There must be a period of thirty days wherein the soldier will reconcile himself to his own passions. He will search his ego and investigate his ambition whether he is really only concerned with the wishful desire, of his lustful aims. Therefore the Torah has a period of waiting—yerech yamim—one month wherein the soldier can realize that this capture is not to be expressed in the terms of pure lust, his actions are not to be demonstrated in the capacity of conquest.

He must express his feeling of conquest in a spiritual and sublime manner, such as bringing tithes unto G-d and sacrificing his material wealth in a spiritual way. The bringing of the first fruit as a sacrifice of man's material plenty and economic abundance to the Priest is a sign of sharing the wealth that a person has accumulated. It is significant because a man who has amassed a great amount of wealth is willing to dedicate and consecrate this material affluence for the sacred purpose of realizing and fulfilling a religious purpose. When a person brings the fruits of plenty, the first of his agricultural crop, the most beautiful of his economic growth to the Kohain, priest, he reads a portion of the Torah. This sacrifice of giving of ourselves is accompanies with a reading of a most significant and elevating statement. It is a declaration of religious purpose, a clarification of a spiritual goal. He reads about the idea of the Jewish historical experience when Israel immersed in bondage engulfed in slavery realized *Exodus* and fulfilled its sense of freedom by breaking the shackles of Egyptian slavery and shaking the yoke of bondage that was placed upon it for many centuries. They persecuted us, they pillaged and plundered us, they ravaged us and laid us in ruin for centuries. Now, when a person offers his fruits that he has grown in Israel, in the land of good and plenty, in the earth from which there flows milk and honey, he must realize that at a time in history he was enslaved, broken, torn assunder, severed from spiritual ties, cut off from cultural creativity, uprooted from material and economic productivity. A man who has reached and is elevated on the social ladder, who makes his mark in society, who walks on the highest rung of the ladder must assert his responsibility for the Priest. He must fulfill a religious obligation and extend his wealth beyond his immediate borders. He must give of himself, divest his great investments to the kohain, to the one who is endorsed with spiritualizing and making the average Jew a more cultural being. Therefore, a man must realize that his economic plenty, material affluence is not to be exercised in a mundane and vain manner. It must be sublimated, transformed, and elevated to a higher ad majestic peak, to a sublime spiritual summit that will make him attain a plateau of performance that is unparalleled in the history of man's quest of ultimate concern with Almighty G-d. Now he must realize as in the festival of Succoth, the ezrach must leave his dwelling, the well-rooted well established citizen of status must remove himself from his castle for a period of a week wherein he will celebrate with all the people on an equal footing in a Succah, in a hut of negligible means, with straw and chaff protecting him. The man of great wealth, great material gain must be subjected to this religious abuse for he must realize that in all his gain, in all his wealth, in all life's abundance, and in all his affluence he's a transient temporary being that has a higher, more elevating, more sublime, more spiritual goal to perform. The affluence of weshoorun must be expressed, enhanced, and advanced in a manner that will mold and shape his cultural and spiritual being. Moses, therefore, admonishes Israel lest they become proud and haughty when they have accumulated a great amount of wealth and luxury for themselves.

Moses admonishes Israel to be cautious, he does not spare words of ethical reproof nor does he limit his great elocution to a feeling of smugness, self-confidence, complacency, and self-righteousness. No, tsoor yludchaw teshee—the rock that has formed you, you forgot, you have abominated G-d with all your transgressions, atrocities and inequities. Moses is perplexed, bewildered about Israel's future. Moses is wondering whether Israel can fulfill its great expectations whether they can summon the courage to perform the goals that it has been assigned, whether it can execute the motifs that it has been delegated. This is the mission, this is the message of Moses, to convey to Israel that it must have courage in times of stress, it must have the conviction to continue in the hour of peril, in the period of torment, in the age of conflict. Wherever they will reside, wherever they will make their abode, wherever they shall dwell, the mission must be upheld. This is the heroic juest, of Hazeenoo and vzos habrachah. If you will harken to the Torah then there will be blessing. The great farewell address uttered by Moses is a tribute for his concern that Israel shall continue in time when history is veiled in a shadow of darkness, clouded in a valley of tears. Then shall Israel experience its finest and heroic hour, to prevail in those eras of peril, to persist when those days are turned to nights. Then the blessing will arise—Hischadshee kanesher noorochee—resurrect and rejuvenate yourself as the burning Phoenix, Knesset Yisrael, realize your commitment, and fulfill your great heritage. Yichayaynoo meeyomayim—During the two millenia of misery, and misfortune, suffering, and agony, the Jews have prevailed, maintained and continued to convey the unique heroic message to the world. Nuflulo sosif, from Israel they declared whatever holocaust will pursue them, whatever travail will transcend upon them, we shall realize a time for uplifting, a moment of salvation, an hour of redemption, and the long day of deliverance is nigh unto G-d. Israel before it has to enter into Canaan and across the Jordan is in a state of solidarity as when the moment of *Exodus* arrived. Thus *Exodus* and entrance are characterized by a unique moment of blissful spiritual experience. They are depicted as in a cultural creative existence, all assembled and unified as one. Before they enter to make their historic heroic mission, that will take them into the glorious glamorous days, and the still silent nights of history, they must experience a moment of solidarity, a time of collective completeness. This will take them and assure them throughout their historic journey. This now is the hour that Moses declares, "Ain kel yeshoorun ashrednaw yisroel." Blessed art thou Israel when you proceed on your historic march to convey and make known, to acknowledge and herald the idea of G-d, the idea of Torah throughout history. The Mountain of Moriah complements the mountain of Sinai, spiritual devotion and cultural creativity are blended in a harmonious unity, formed in a collective oneness to express the idea of G-dliness, the supreme sovereign rule of Almighty G-d throughout the entire earth, throughout the whole universe. Israel is armed with its heritage of massoretic courage which will maintain them on the battlefield, comfort them on the plains of battle.

Joshua is now charged with the task of directing the Jews in battle. He's designated with the mission of conquering Canaan, assigned with the task of dividing the land for Israel, for its tribes. The conquest of Canaan is brought about by Rachav, who aids and assists the spies who were sent out by Joshua on an expedition to observe the military strength of Jericho. The Mraglim are spared by Rachav's kindness. What is the lesson we can derive and what is the inference that we may deduce from this assistance by Rachav? That our mission to convey to the world must be accompanied and accomodated with the help and assistance of the universal community. The particular, personalized, private community of Israel does not maintain itself in a vacuum, in a void, in a special relationship, isolated and segregated from the world at large, or removed and remote from the mainstream of general civilization. The Bible is viable because it continues to communicate throughout the entire world. It is within the world that we grow, and amidst the tensions and entanglements of world politics that Israel's unique dimension of a nation assumes its special character. Rachan therefore is that symbol of generating the universal community to come and assist the particular. We enlist the aid of Rachav and we also enlist the aid of the daughter of Pharaoh to bring about redemption and salvation for the particular, personal, private community of Israel. We enlist the support of the general, total and world community. Redemption of Israel is brought about also by Cyrus. Korash-Cyris is expressly stated as G-d's anointed. Therefore we observe that redemption of Israel, its continuity for timeless history is expressly derived from the product of the entire world historic scene. We do not live in a vacuum, we do not reside in the wilderness, on the mountain tops or in a distant forest concealed from the historic movement of worldly progress. We are not encased in a cover, shielded from the occurrences and events of world dynamic history. We have to live within and participate amidst the world community. Therefore, the Prophet tells us that Jewish history is molded against the background of total history, within the mainstream of humanity. We cannot divorce ourselves or become disassociated from this supreme sublime task. In all our ghettos wherein we were expelled from the world arena, made isolated and looked upon as a pariah in the panorama of world history, we have extricated ourselves from the plight of world strangulation, we have not submitted ourselves to become ensnared in the pitfall of standing aside as a spectator. Although for many centuries and at many times we were pillaged and plundered, ravaged and ruined, nevertheless the historic call for heroic Judaism has made its claim and stamped its indelible imprint on humanity. The world community cannot extricate itself from Israel and Israel is not likely to isolate itself from the nations of the world. After the battle of Ei, when Israel experienced defeat, they asked G-d for the reason. They were bewildered as to the reason of their failure. Why should they experience such a setback after G-d had performed great miracles for them? The Jews had never lost on the battlefield, defeating such great Empires as Seechao and Og, annihilating the Amalekites, routing the Midianites. Why now, after they had successfully desolated Jerich had they encountered such a misfortune? The answer was given because Uchan defied the ban that Joshua issued that the Jews should not take any share of the booty, they should not plunder the spoils that they captured on the battlefield. This misfortune that they were confronted with was a true test of the solidarity and unity of the Jewish community. It was an epic-making event in the unfolding drama of Jewish history, that to ensure the survival of Judaism, to maintain the continuity of its heroic destiny, they must act as a unified whole, structured and rooted in accord, not in discord. Uchan, the prophets state committed a maal, an atrocity with his treacherous act. He concealed his wicked intent to grasp hold of the spoil, to grab the booty on the battlefield. This was a treacherous act because it denoted Uchan's lust and desire for power. The battle of Canaan, the conquest of Israel was to be a spiritual one, that it was a religious war, not one to gain spoils, to expect material booty. Therefore Uchan was destroyed because he entertained the idea to disrupt the harmony of the group. The quest for power, the search for pride must be stripped from any cultural creative mission. The first conquest of Jericho was t obe devoid of power, divested of conquering pride. Therefore the Jews encountered defeat at Ei.

After they had repented, they routed the Canaanite armies until Joshua prayed that the sun may remain standing—shemesh bgibon dom vyorayach bemek ayawlon—now that Joshua had once again asserted his marvelous strategic exploits at the battlefield, when he had regained the drive to generate the excellent courageous military warfare, he utters a poem and expresses his miraculous conquests—that the sun should remain standing and this phrase of poetry is interpreted and inserted because military conquest is not the aim and objective of Israel. It is only to perform the central goal of conveying the idea of G-dliness. It is only to maintain the unique sovereignty of Israel. Likewise, after Moses had achieved his military aim and objective at conquering Seechon and Og, there is an insertion of poetry when he proclaims keep aish hawtsaw micheshbon uchlaw armnosedaw, a fire has ascended from chesbon, destroyed and consumed its palaces, and masterful architectural structures.

Thus, the song of Deborah, the song of David, and the song of Moses at the splitting of the sea are expressions of G-d's intervention and G-d's miraculous accomplishments using Israel as His tool, as His mission to convey His glory. Am zoo yawtsartaw lee theelawsee yisapayroo, that this nation I have created unto me to express my glory, lichvodee bawrawsiv ytsartiv af assesiv —for my glory I have created him, formed him, even fashioned him, to express My glory, to proclaim My grandeur to the nations of the world.

David then who is depicted as the chanter par excellence, the singer of G-d's heavenly muse is simultaneously acclaimed as the great warrior of Israel, the man who established the boundary lines—firm geographical locations to assure the peace and enhance the political stability of Israel. "Noom hagever hookam ul" the voice of the human who has overcome the obstacles and championed the problems, encountered the paradoxes of life, and confronted the conflicts of human destine sings. David, therefore, is the one who sings G-d's heavenly song because the great warrior is overcome with the mystical and sublime spiritual feeling, the sense of elevation that to attain G-d's heavenly plateau, to mount the summit of his ultimate religious experience man must expand beyond the finite, limited and quantified material drive of pure military conquest. Nkee kpayim oovur layuuv—who can ascend to the mountain of G-d? Who can prevail in the place of this sanctity? Who can reach the great heights of G-d's elevated and sublime region? The one who is pure of heart, pure of hand, free from iniquity, devoid of transgression. Therefore poetry is the result of man's answer to why he has to entertain military battles, why must he be engulfed in a paralysis of power, that he must drive with fury, with his passionate pride. The why of this drive resounds in the quiet echo of "i'kee kpayim" of "zee door dorshuv mvakshay pawnechaw yaakov selah"—Every generation men rise up, notions confront and the world civilization aims to submerge and subdue Israel. The nations of the world "rugshoo" have clamoured and gathered together to overcome an overwhelm Jacob, to ensnare him in the path of moral abyss, to entrap him in the pitfall of spiritual degradation and cultural depravity. They have assembled in every generation to uproot and annihilate, to pillage and plunder, ravage and ruin, desolate and decimate the community of Israel. Zion, however, reverberates with defiance, resounds with fury that we shall forever stand, we shall forever prevail and continue to realize the time when "nedeevay amim nesaphod," the princes of teh world shall be gathered together to honor the G-d of Abraham, to give homage and express their esteem for Almighty G-d." Kee l'Elohim mgeenay aretz mod nalaw," for Almighty G-d has become exalted and his Kingship reigns and endures forever. The nations of the world shall sing and exclaim in a proud and grandeur voice the praise of G-d. Let us go and arise "koomah v'naleh," let us arise to the house of Jacob, to the mountain of the L-rd for he shall teach us in His ways, He shall guide us and instruct us, He shall develop and encourage us in the path of spiritual progress. No longer shall we utilize our brain power, our creativity, and our productivity for military exploits. Rather we shall become one universal peaceful community, enriched with a sublime, harmonious, blissful religious experience.

Joshua dispatches Pinchas to act as a delegate to restore the peace and harmony between the tribes. There is rumor of an insurrection led by the Reubenites who reside on the other side of the Jordan. Pinchas therefore is sent to quell the alleged rebellion, to subside any friction that could arise from the geographical separation. Therefore, Pinchas who was the agent for the atonement of the desecration of the spiritual sanctity of Israel with his vengeance to assert the dignity of G-d, has now assumed another character, one of peace and spiritual diplomacy. The Reubenites assured him that they were not concerned in stimulating any conflict. They were, however, only interested in preserving a monument for their children and generations that would arise afterward. Pinchas is satisfied with the explanation and the revolution is abated.

Joshua, we see, is the general of peaceful harmony, as in *Numbers* when he declares unto Moses, "My master Moses, imprison them," cannot be complacent and over-confident when it comes to any stirring of revolution or simmering of rebellion. His legislation, his leadership is characterized with the continuity of peace and harmony, a spiritual blissful relationship between the leader and the led. Thus Auchun is dispensed of and his treacherous act is exposed because he plotted to ensnare the Jews in the pitfall of lustful act for power. Then Pinchas is sent on a troubleshooting expedition to reaffirm Joshua's confidence that no rebellion has come about. Even the Gibeonites were learn asked the Elders to become part of the Jewish community, although they were condoned by the Elder statesmen. Joshua expressed his anger that he was not considered in resolving the mysterious issue of the Gibeonites. However, Joshua placed them in the lower rung of Jewish life; as hewers of wood and drawers of water that they may not plot any insurrection in supplanting the confidence of Israel.

Thus Joshua was buried in "timnas cheres," the picture of sunlight, as his character was depicted like the streaming, blazing, glorious sunlight. There was no dimness during his career as general. There were no clouds of despair that could hover over his tenure of leadership. Joshua however admonishes the Jews and warns them in the strongest terms and in fact draws a covenant that they shall continue in the path of Moses and himself, that the covesant of Jishua is an expression of the heroic mission of continuity, the timeless quest of performing our historic destiny, the ageless task of exercising the courageous contribution that we have to convey to civilization at large. This is the message of Joshua in the Mosaic creed; they must uphold the tenets of the faith to assure their triumphant lasting quality on the earth, the promised land that G-d bestowed o their forefathers.

The era of the *Judges* come about after Joshua, and is filled with conflict and controversy, overwhelmed with the ups and downs of the seemingly periods of rest at interludes to the almost ceaseless conflict that engaged the Jews and confronted the Israelites on the battleground. The Phillistines, the Canaanites and all the countries around them sought to sweep them off their promised land. Individual heroes arise, national heroes are established. Osneecl ben knass captures land, Aihood ben gayrah slays Eglon, Shumga ben Aanus is a hero. These are all singular events that cut across the continuous struggle for preserving the Jewish sovereignty on its Promised Land. Devorah is characterized as the judge of Israel, the singer of the melodious muse of the heavenly song that binds nature unto G-d, that sublimates nature to work as an agent of G-d's miraculous power. Eretz raashaw ham shemay im ntufoo—the entire earth trembled and the heavens were clouded with G-d's awesome conquest of the universe. Min shemayim nilchamoo—from the heavens above they fought against Sisera to overwhelm the enemies of G-d, to vanquish and subdue those who arise to submerge and overpower the great spiritual sovereignty of Israel's right for preserving its destiny.

Thus as in the song of Moses, nature is formed to serve G-d. We must transform and elevate the powers of nature to uplift our personal character, to aspire as religious beings, creatures of G-d's handiwork, expressing His glory, singing of His grandeur, praising His miraculous intervention, lauding the works of G-d. Therefore, sehaylee lanvayhoo—this is my G-d and I shall ador him, the G-d of my father and I shall exalt Him. Suglimating nature is the manifest expression of exalting Almighty G-d.

The parable of Jatham and the riddle of Samson is an expression of wisdom in those days when the *Judges* governed. It is a spiritual declaration of understanding G-d in the nomadic environment that govern the entire society wherein Israel dwelt. Samson, however who is endowed with unique strength is characterized as being the great heroic conqueror of the Philistines. He is described as the champion who toyed with the Philistines and made mockery of Israel's enemies. Samson was born of parents who at first were childless. Then the angel appeared to Manoach and his wife declaring that Samson shall be a Nazarite abstaining from wine and intoxicating beverages and no razor shall touch his hair. This then is the symbol wherein Samson shall lead the Jews against the Philistines individually. This individual heroic action is characteristic during the period of judges by judges except for the battle of Deborah wherein tens of thousands of Jews assembled to fight, wage battle against Canaanite tribes. There were individual heroes, heroes who ventured against the Philistines on their own, on an independent course. Samson is destined for leadership by his sign of the nazir abstaining from earthly pleasures and removing himself, disassociating himself from the passionate pursuit of lustful behavior. However, Samson is ensnared by Delilah. Entrapped by the Philistine maiden he cannot extricate himself from sliding into the pitfall of spiritual abyss. Nevertheless, he summons all his strength and gathers his energy to express his firm devotion that although he has failed in leading the Jews for he has succumbed to the passions of his boastful energetic prowess he exercises a true religious repentance at his end wherein he slays more Philistines in his death than during his life at conquering of the Philistines in battle. Samson is a Nazarite born out of strength to uplift his people, to elevate them from the pitfall of Philistine subjection. He is the symbol of Jewish external heroic conquest on the battleground. He is the sign of the Jewish external drive to overwhelm and overpower the Philistines on the battlefield. Born out of a state of pure sanctity wherein no razor was to touch his hair nor could he drink wine, he was destined to be the champion of Israel, the conqueror of the Philistines. This abstension from physical drives, from the pursuit of material splendor was to enhance his external gevoorah, his ability to conquer and his genius to annihilate the oppressors of Israel.

Samson is the symbol of the striking sunlight of Israel, when Israel assumes its glory, attires itself in grandeur, arrays itself in beauty to overcome and overwhelm those that aspire to submerge her in the pitfall of spiritual abyss. Delilah, therefore symbolizes night fall, lailah, the darkness that hovers over spiritual splendor and seeks to engage and overtake it in the stand of amidst a veil which demoralizes and degrades its great unique historic message. Thus Delilah momentarily engulfed Samson and created a pitfall where Samson slid down and was not able to elevate and extricate himself from the plight of his mundane material passion and became allured by the beauty and fragrance of Delilah. However, when the moment of truth had arrived, the trying time when Samson realized that all his strength was evaporating, when the end was about to occur lest the Jews would surrender and the Philistines would overtake and rout Israel from its promised land, then Samson with a last breath, with a last gasping desire of spiritual fervor expresses his supreme wish, and the spark of his dim sunlight comes glaring forth, bursting through to uplift and extricate his people from the plight of Philistine oppression.

Samuel in contrast is born as a Nazarite, destined as a leader who will abstain from food and drink that is abhorrent to the spiritually sanctified person. No razor shall touch his hair. Samuel is also depicted as a man who is consecrated and dedicated unto G-d all his life. However, his gevoorah, strength, his vigor and diligence is an internal growth, internal development, internal comprehension of G-d's wonderful, miraculous, and supernatural deeds to mankind.

SAMUEL

Chapter 5

Samuel, unlike Moses, has a different message to convey. His prophecy has assumed a character of confronting and challenging mankind within crises of culture, within conflict of creative and productive social development. Samuel is the prophet who merges above and beyond conflict against the background of confrontation, within the context of man's ever growing tensions, ever burdening dilemmas that engulf his very existence and overwhelm his very being. Moses is delegated and designated for the noble task and majestic mission of elevating his people and extricating Israel from the yoke of oppression, from the shackles of slavery, from the tyranny of bondage. Samuel has quite another task to perform, quite another mission to accomplish, and his goal is created from circumstances that are wholly dissimilar to that of Moses. Samuel's prophecy merges from Israel's surrender to passion and he arises from the environment of Israel's succumbing to the alluring and seductive material splendor of the Philistines. "Hence Israel shall be confounded on the battlefield, confused on the battleground, and the Ark of the L-rd," Samuel declares, "will be taken away." Samuel conveys his message to Aylee, that Israel shall go down to defeat on the battlefield, Israel who was proud and glorious shall encounter failure and disaster on the battlefield, on the plains of military conflict. In the hills and the highways of strategic warfare, they shall experience doom and disaster. Samuel's prophecy expresses a new message for Israel. It is designed to convey that Israel's continuity is predicated on the overcoming of its obstacles and sidestepping the barriers of spiritual decay, cultural degradation and moral depravity. Israel must arise from the pitfall of spiritual abyss if she is to overcome the barrier of isolation and segregation from Almighty G-d. Aylee is overwhelmed at Samuel's prophecy. When the news is returned that Israel has encountered failure, experienced disaster at the battlefield, and that the Ark of the L-rd has been taken in captivity, the pride of Israel has been subdued, the glory of Jacob has succumbed to the lustful and licentious Philistines who engage in material pride, who are immersed in sensual splendor, then Aylee falls down, collapses, and Samuel must take over the helm of spiritual leadership. Samuel now ushers in a new dimension in Israel's cultural historic destiny. With Samuel there comes about the advent of a new era in its intellectual creative productivity, a new age in its intellectual spiritual development. Samuel is the prophet who will now confront, challenge and express his distaste and abhorrent discontent for evil practice. Samuel will now be ahe standard bearer against atrocity, the spokesman against inequity, the statesman for excellence that will ridicule and deprimand, reprove and serve as a moral lecturer for the entire community of Israel. He will stand against the King, he will arise to lecture and instruct, guide and direct Israel along the course of spirituality, on the rugged road of spiritual redemption. Israel now has experienced a new age, a new period, a horizon beyond the cloud of despair, a ray of sun beyond the dim dusk of darkness that hovers upon defeat when men become disillusioned at being annihilated on the battleground. Samuel speaks out against all. He is the prophet who has achieved as ultimate concern with G-d because he is only preoccupied with the truth, he is only involved in study, only immersed in the development of law, in the nurturing of cultural creativity, in the growth of spiritual spontaneity. "Kach meekooblanee meebais deeno shel shmooel hurumawsee," declares the Talmud, so have I received and been instructed from the court of Samuel. Chana prepared a mayeel katan, a small mantle, in which Samuel was garbed. His internal growth development and maturity was garbed in a small mantle. Even the cloth that covered his body, the robe that was his reverential dress was small in stature. He did not perform with external glamour nor did he wear a halo that would express a vain and mundane attitude of seeking glory, searching after pride. The prophet—nuvee—Samuel is born out of a sense of physical and military defeat. There is chaos and no instructive movement in Israel. Ayn chawzon nifrutz, no message has sprouted forth, no vision has arisen to extricate Israel from the plight of its material pitfalls. Therefore Samuel arises to admonish, reprimand, and to administer education to Israel. Samuel warns the people against monarchical rule, and a great storm, a downpour of rain comes upon the land in summertime when rainfall is non-occurrent, when the earth should blossom with sunlight. Samuel exposes the wrath of G-d by symbolizing to Israel that the rainfall in summertime, out of season, out of region is a bad omen for their distrust and disregard for Almighty G-d's precepts and concepts. "Israel," declares Samuel, "must not rely on physical power, kingly rule, regal governmental legislation that seeks to corrupt, endeavors to corrode, an dis in its essential form chaotic in nature, destructive in action. Your daughters will be taken away as part of the king's harem, your sons will have to go out on the battlefield, your vineyards will be confiscated." Samuel presents to the people the entire picture of monarchical rule, where kings exploit with their whimsical passion and domineering power they shall subdue the people, conquer the masses, and exact great levies, high tolls from the country. This is not the way to G-dliness; this is not the road to aspire toward His sublime spiritual summit; this is not the map wherein one plots out an itinerant journey to reach upward, to leap across the conflicts and challenges that confront mankind on his arduous journey and most difficult task of maintaining his survival and continuing along the course of cultural creativity and spiritual productivity. Therefore, Samuel is the one who rebels against the aristocracy of wealth; he revolts against the elite of power; he is the arch critic of the wealthy class who are intent upon making the people conform, making the masses subservient to the will of their power. "The people," Samuel declares, "are but a tool of the upper class."

Saul was disobedient to Samuel and rejected Samuel's orders to annihilate and uproot the Amalekites. Therefore Samuel communicates Saul's doom and despair. Saul will no longer sit on the throne of royalty, he shall surrender his seat of glory to one who is more valiant in battle, more deeply devoted and dedicated to the service of G-d. That was David. Saul haunted David all his life and at teh end Saul capitulated, surrendered on the battlefield of Gilboa, whereas Samuel's prediction was inevitable. Saul who had disobeyed from harkening unto the word of G-d had to relinquish his royal grandeur, he had to depart and step aside for someone who was greater, someone who had deeper vision for the everlastingtimeless quality of Israel. For the royal seat of David that was envisaged by G-d will forever remain and shall always retain its spiritual heroic destiny. Samuel then is the adversary of monarchical rule; he is the opponent of man's dependence on physical prowess, on his ability for military exploits on the battlefield. Samuel admonishes Saul because he did not adhere to G-d's commandments. Saul was not obedient to G-d's precept in destroying the Amalekites who sought to eradicate, uproot and annihilate Israel. Saul rather had pity and he showed mercy for the Amalekites, he rescued Agog its king. Then Samuel slew Agog declaring to Saul that his kingdom, his reign would terminate; it would be delivered to one who is more favored in the eyes of G-d.

Saul pursues David and seeks to slay him at every opportunity. Saul is overcome with a jealous drive, a morose ambition to encounter David had overcome him. David however slips away at all moments of confrontation. David in fact does not want to execute any physical injury on the anointed of G-d, the appointed deliverer of Israel. Thus Saul is depicted in one great moment, from his shoulders and upward he is greater than all of Israel. However once he assumes his monarchical rule, once he is garbed in the regal attire of kingly splendor then he becomes debased in his actions and depraved in his moral attitudes. Saul slays everyone who seeks the friendship of David. Evil talk is a daily occurrence and the kohanim and the Gibeonites are slain in order to preserve Saul's jealous anger, his infatuated delight to prey upon innocent David who is truly the annointed one of G-d. Samuel's prophecy against the monarchy is an inevitable truth. Israel's experience of aspiring to be one of the nations, to have the same governmental splendid irder as the non-Jewish environment to indulge in the luxury of haughty and prideful might is a failure and a shocking episode in the historical movement of Israel's dynamic history. From now on and henceforth the prophet will become the adversary of the king. The man of intellect will arise against those who are boastful and prideful of their great material affluence, of their great economic abundance, of their great accumulation of wealth, spoils gold and silver. The mission of the prophet henceforth is to acknowledge the fact that Israel is not like the other nations. "Neeyeh kchol hogoyim bais yisroel hawyaw loseeyeh—declares the prophet. Shall we be like all the other nations, never shall it come to be. With an iron hand shall I rule you, with fury and might shall I govern Israel, declares Almighty G-d." This message is conveyed to the prophet, to warn Israel, to admonish Jacob that they must adhere and conform to the will of G-d. Elijah encounters the Nveeay habaal on Mount Carmel. Nathan encounters David who indulges in illicit sexual relations with Bethsheba. Even Oozee yawhoo who built strong towers, fortified cities, became a leper because he sought to defile the word of G-d, he sought to deny the will of the prophet. He wanted to assume pride, the pride of priesthood. He was not content with his regal power. Rather he wanted to assume more power, he wanted to become the omnipotent ruler and the dictator, that he alone would issue orders, he alone would advance proclamations. What should be the protocol and design of the cultural climate of opinion is to be dictated by Oozeeyawhoo. Therefore, he became a leper. The entire earth shook because mighty power is only unto G-d, is reserved for the Almighty One. Alone we cannot assume total power, we cannot assert our animalistic drives beyond infinite boundaries, beyond unquenchable dreams. Yehoshafat who likewise judged Israel with great skill, intellectual acumen, with creative genius, was foiled because he made a pact engaging in an unholy alliance with Achab who was the abominable heathen worshipper and was not the proper ally for a king of righteous acts, righteous deeds and noble performances.

The history of monarchy therefore is a history, a record of savage, cruel, brutal acts, failure in establishing the perfect, noble majestic order of G-d's kingship, G-d's kingdom on the universe. Thus physical strength and intellectual creativity are severed and broken in Israel. The prophet wars against the king. Only destruction, discard, and disharmony is the outgrowth and development of this new governmental dimension. The order that it assumes to maintain is chaotic in nature, corrosive in structure. Only after the destruction of the Temple when Israel is stripped of its spiritual beauty and religious splendor were the two reunited and once again emerged as one force in the collective community of Israel. Thus, yehoshooa ben yehotzuduk and Zeroobuvel ben shaltiel are unified in one motif to perpetuate the continuity of Israel, to restore its original glory, to replace its ruins and desolation with evergrowing vitality and rejuvenating dynamic spirit. Exra and Nehemiah are the classic synthesis of strength, material outward growth, material external beauty, the glamour of Israel, the pride of Jacob with the intellectual, spiritual inner development and inner glow that is to serve as Israel's vital force for generations to come. Samuel therefore, ushers in the heroic age of speaking out against tyranny, voicing disapproval against oppression, demonstrating with the articulate creative ability of prophecy that Israel's future does not lie in material strength, in physical prowess of exploits on the battlefield. Israel's glory is in upholding the spirit of G-d, in maintaining the cultural creativity of its law, in abiding by the precepts of G-d, in conforming, enhancing and advancing the word of G-d.

David, who was annointed by Samuel to fulfill the spiritual void and moral vacuum left by Saul has also encountered much criticism from the prophets, Nathan and Gad. When we contrast the character of David prior to his reign and his personal development after he was annointed we can ascertain a sharp, clear, and definite distinction. Before he was elected to serve on the royal seat of the Davidic dynasty, he was the General who slew Goliath, he was the true champion of Israel of whom was sung: Saul smote in teh thousands and David in the tens of thousands. David was appreciated by the mases of Israel and he was highly revered and respected by Jonathan, the son of Saul. When Samuel came to annoint David as King, he looked at all of Yeeshai's sons before he came to David. Samuel was under the impression that David was not to be selected as the Supreme Ruler of Israel. Why did Samuel entertain this misgiving? Why was he misled to think that David was not to be annointed? True David was the youngest son. However, even younger sons were elected as Supreme Rules and were delegated with supreme tasks and highly essential missions with the development of creative Israel. Why then was Samuel in doubt whether David can truly be called the leader of Israel, the ruler of Jacob? Now Samuel who admonished Saul for his wrong doings, and evil acts, atrocious behavior, neglectful character in fulfilling his obligations and performing his duties as a King was perplexed whether David also would line up to the expectations of the true monarch, of the truly revered religious regal leader. David was blessed with external strength, beauty, and glamour. The maidens of Israel attested to that fact, that David was handsome in stature and aristocratic in appearance. Would David succumb to the passions of monarchal power when he would become the appointed leader of Israel? Would David fulfill the covenant of Israel unto G-d, or would David bc compliant to his own malicious ambitions and lustful tendencies for self-aggrandizement self-gratification? David before he assumed the monarchy was a symbol of Israel's endurance under pressure. David's character was truly splendid, magnificent and superior in spiritual quality. He had the opportunity to slay Saul; he could have grasped the monarchal rule much sooner; he could have overwhelmed and overpowered Saul's beleaguered and tired army. David had ambushed the oppressive Saul and in reasonable terms he could have easily rationalized his drive for power, his anxiety for assuming the pride of royal glory.

Rather, David waited with persistent patience and painstaking perseverance against the oppressive abuse heaped upon him by the annointed Saul who was destined for failure because of his wanton jealousy and inane anxiety to reap vengeance against the young David. The story of Abigail, who beguiled David into her request that David should not slay Naval who was wicked and a treacherous man. David who had bestowed great kindness to Naval and tended his flock with honor and care was not repayed with that kindness and friendliness of Naval who should have acted in good faith toward David. David at once charges down with his army, swoops down upon the territor yof Naval to conquer, overpower and overwhelm him. However, Abigail reconciles his anger and comforts him with gifts of food and wine. She also requites him that in due time my lord will be uplifted from his peril and extricated from the plight of pursuit in which he is presently engulfed. David is obedient to the wishes of Abigail. He is truly the man who can reconcile his external gevoorah (strength), glory, glitter, and glow with his internal chesed, intellectual creative kindness and majestic noble qualities that must be harmonized if he is to exercise the truly exemplary champion of Israel. When David also was pitched in battle against the Philistines who ransacked communities of Israel, he made it a law that those who protected the families of his army were to share alike in the spoils that were captured by the men who were involved in the actual combat. Thus, we observe that David was concerned and not aloof to the miral responsibility that was placed upon his shoulders. He was keenly aware of the obligations that were expected of him to perform as leader and general of the men whom he governed. However, when we encounter David as the King in the *Second Samuel* we observe almost a radical transformation in his character, a distinct change in that epoch making man who was the annointed of G-d, the elected of Israel. Now we see David slipping into the pitfalls of spiritual abyss, sliding into the dense darkness which encounters those who commit atrocities and transgress against the word of G-d. David, when he was pursued by Saul in flight from the Israelite King was the spiritual champion of justice. He was painstaking patient, persistent and persevering in his firm dedication and full devotion oward G-d and men. He was cognizant of his role that was required of him to perform both as military strategist and spiritual leader. He was not detoured nor did he digress from the path of advancing toward spiritual service of G-d. He was always aware of moral responsibility and spiritual obligation, fulfilling and participating with the people and for the people. He was not fooled into the passion of subjecting himself to his own physical exploits and prowess, to the pride and glory of his own physical exploits and military conquests. Rather David was merely concerned with the spiritual security and economic safety, economic welfare and well-being of his people. However, after the slaying of Saul on Mount Bilboa there is a new view that one experiences in David. He is changed, his character altered, his posture has assumed quite another pose. Almost imediately he falls into the charms of Bathsheba, casting Uriah into the hands of the enemy that he may be slain to permit David legitimately to take Bathsheba for a wife. This rationalization is abhorred and detested by the prophet Nathan. David later openly admits to his blatant transgression against G-d. This is the arena of royal power that begins to unfold on the path of disintegration, dissolution and discontent. David is now like Saul, seeking after his own vain pleasures. He is only concerned with material gain, material success, and material adventure. He is no longer interested and involved in the spiritual adventure of G-d. This transgression, atrocity, and inequity on behalf of David commences the downfall or disintegration of the Davidic dynasty. Soon after Amnan and Tamar are engaged in an incestual adulterous act that is a flagrant violation of the religious norm. Abshalom takes vengeance on behalf of Tamar and slays Amnon. The grudge that Abshalom hears against Amnon is depicted quite ostensively and it affords an illuminating insight into the character of Abshalom who was later to arouse the Israelites against his father, David, to lure them and steal the heart of the people in attempting to overthrow his father, David, Sheva ben Bichree is another leader who seeks to lead an insurrection, rebellion, a revolt against David. These expressions of distrust, dislike against David are a result of that atrocity that David committed. It exposes the character of a Kind and it expresses the deplorable corruptive atmosphere that is all pervasive when the king assumes his powerful seat of honor, his glorious throne of pride. David was even sympathetic toward Abshalom who nearly uprooted and annihilated his army. David expressed excessive sympathy about the illicit child whom Bathsheba bore to him. He was overcome with an overemphasis of pity because he was prone to be induced and seduced by the passions and pride that ensnare one who has encountered failure. One who has experienced disillusion when he has ascended to great glory, to an immense peak of glamour cannot readily succumb to any obstacle or pitfall that is placed in his path. David who has arisen to such a seat of power, such a throne of glory cannot be consoled when he has encountered misery, misfortune. He cannot be comforted when he has experienced doom, disaster, and despair because military power is futile and fatal. It does not enhance the spiritual character nor does it advance the moral integrity of the person. Thus David who had experienced glamour of conquest, glory of military success asks his chief general Joab to take a census. Joab complains bitterly. Why must the king entertain such a foolish idea? G-d has blessed his people with great multitudes of pipulation, with great material success. Why now must the king exercise such an inane notion? David was overcome with his military exploits. He was overpowered by his own passion, enamored with the great glory that was expressed in the royal Davidic splendor. G-d however reconciles David and when David buys the threshing floor of the Aravnaw hayevoosee as a place for an altar to sacrifice unto G-d, the wrath of G-d subsides, the sin of David is atoned. What is inherent in this purchase, in this purchase of Aravnaw the Yevoosite and what is so significant that G-d's wrath which was kindled against David is dissolved? Why does G-d now bestow once again his grave on David? What is the significance behind this sale? Furthermore, why is David reluctant to accept this parcel of land as a gift that Aravaneh would eagerly be pleased to bestow upon David as a token of friendship? Why also when Abraham declares to Ephron the Hitite that he would like to buy a parcel of land to bury Sarah his beloved wife, Ephron was almost insistent that Abraham should accept the parcel gratis? The quest for power and the thirst and drive for greed and pride is an insatiable instinct of man's behavior and attitude. In maintaining and participating in life, renunciation of this gratifying passion is a supreme desire of the ethical imperatve. If man is to elevate himself above pride, uplift himself beyond the anxiety of his animal sensuous quest then he must relinquish and renunciate the ego gratifying ambition of assuming a character that corrupts and corrodes his divine image and spiritual perspective. Thus Abraham who had accumulated such an enormous amount of wealth, who was enriched with so much plenty for G-d had fulfilled his material and economic prosperity beyond the usual limits of riches, had increased his material resources to such great propirtions, nevertheless, had to confront a unique challenge.

Abraham, therefore, was onfronted with a new unique challenge in his evergrowing religious development, in his ever spontaneous spiritual quest for searching and driving to the ultimate plateau of ascertaining G-d's grace. Now in time of strife and struggle, in strain and stress when he was under such intense frustration, and overcome with the remorse and grief that was inflicted upon him with the death of his beloved wife, Sarah, he nevertheless confined his will and restricted his desire to acquire the land by the means of a granted gift. A gift bestowed upon Abraham would have manifestly exposed his character as being one who is merely concerned and only preoccupied with the accession of wealth, with the grasping of territory for his own self glorification and agrandizement. Such a self-righteous act was scorned by Abraham because his character was spiritually pure and free from smug and self-complacent blemishes that creep up upon man's soul and corrupt the very vitality, vigor and veracity of his divinely noble and G-dly majestic soul. Therefore, Abraham renunciates the present that Ephron request of him to accept as symbolic of bonafide friendship. Rather Abraham is content with a simply purchase because the method of acquisition demonstrates the capacity of Abraham to conform as a simple citizen with rules and regulations like an average man without any special privileges of nobility, without any preference toward his great accumulation of wealth, power and good name that was attributed to him. Now David also had to become exposed to this unique challenge. Before the great pestilence that brought about David's reconciliation with G-d the purchase of the threshing floor of Aravneh Hayevoosee for a sacrificial altar David was to request of G-d that he, David might build a house, a palace for the worship of G-d, a place of spiritual meeting, where men could come together and pray with unity toward G-d and toward their fellow man. "G-d," complains David, "has no resting place, no dwelling house wherein His name could be magnified and glorified to all the nations of the world, that civilization should adorn the splendor of G-d, that the community of the entire world would give homage and express their appreciation for the miraculous and supernatural glory of G-d." G-d's answer was to declare unto David that his wish would be granted though not in his lifetime. "Your hands are filled with blood," contends the prophet in conveying his response to David's plea, "your son Solomon will fulfill the noble task and majestic mission of this sublime purpose." Therefore, David who had experienced the failure of not being able to perform the mission of his heart's desire, to adorn G-d in splendored majesty that all the nations of the world would testify to the sublimating and transforming character of wealth and pride into the holy and pure sanctifying aspect of G-d's supreme universal sovereignty. David perhaps was overcome with remorse and filled with regret, perplexed with his ineptitude and inadequate quality to execute the great mission that he had set out to accomplish. When famine struck the earth, when hunger and pestilence came about, David was evermore overcome with wonder and grief, anxiety and stress for the friendship of Almighty G-d. "Let me fall at the hand of G-d," declares David at the agony of the great poet's ecstatic emotional experience unto G-d. David therefore was not concerned in being granted a gift by Aravneh, he was not interested in exalting his pride, in manifesting his ego on behalf of his covenant unto G-d. Rather a simple purchase would restore the wrath of G-d and subside the anger of Almighty G-d. The purchase would symbolize that David is now concerned only with his expression of fervor and spiritual sanctification of his own character unto G-d. David is not anxious to acquire this property because of his superior statesman-like qualities. His ambition and request is to fulfill the desire of G-d. David realizes the error of acquiring lustful pride. The ambition of greed and power is vain and futile, it can only lead to disintegration and depravity, the soul is torn, the spirit is splintered because of man's vain, inane, mundane drives to acquire power. Thus we observe how monarchal rule leads to internal strife and external chaos. Even with Solomon who built the temple, erected the Tabernacle of G-d, constructed a dwelling place for the Almighty incurred failure when he became heatedly involved and intensively exposed to the passions of his pursuit after pleasure. Even Solomon could not extricate himself from the pitfalls of lustful pride, of acquiring the beauty that misleads and misguides one along the path toward approaching G-d. Thus Solomon and David, who both were noble in their attempts to become exalted spiritual beings experienced immense degradation and internal dispair. The moment of torment came to them because all power corrupts, it uproots the personality and transplants it from the spiritual celestial sublime summit of G-dliness, to the lowly dense darkness of despair and disastrous despondency veiled in the horrors and tragedies of failure, misery and misfortune.

As the prophet declares, "Awroor Ashoor shayvet apee oomateh zamlchapee, cursed is Assyria, the rod of My wrath and the stick of My scorn placed in My hand. Ashur's instrument of power, its immense persecution of lands that it has plundered, pillaged, ravaged and ruined, its essential role of the desolation and decimation of the various countries and communities is only a pawn in the hand of G-d. Neboochadnetzar, the mighty king of Babylon sitting on the throne of his glorious empire, vexing his power, persecuting, and punishing with infinite anguish and agony is called a servant of G-d. These rulers who exercise military exploits on the battlefield are only tools placed in the hand of G-d to perform a temporary mission to cleanse the nations of the dross that has been formed by their corrosive culture, lveeyawsun zoo yawtzartaw lsachaik bo, the Leviathans that lie in ambush that plan and plot to ensnare and entrap are only brought upon this earth as a mission of cathartic purpose, to cleanse the nations of their iniquities that they have perpetuated and committed against G-d. Thus Cyrus who is the Messianic symbol of G-d, who performs a noble and majestic task is to elevate the sublime mission of Israel from the despair of Diaspora. Both Solomon and David who encountered despair in their kingdom and experienced a certain degree of disaster in their reign as sovereign leaders of Israel were aware of their entrapment and were concerned that others should not become ensnared likewise in the pitfall spiritual abyss. David begins his psalms declaring, "Blessed is the man who has not walked in the council of the wicked, in the patios of the transgressors he has not stood, and in the accompaniment of scoffers he has not placed his abode, for only in the law of G-d is his desire and in the L-rd he shall dwell day and night." David was well aware of the entrapments, ensnarements, obstacles, and pitfalls that lie in the path of spiritual progress, that grasp a man and engulf him in the sea of submerging stress and ceaseless agony, that ends in frightful calamity. Solomon was also a keen observer of this cruel fact, of this crucial element in an's life that creeps up upon him, and overwhelm him, and encompasses his very being. My son, if transgressors shall seduce you and induce you to stray from the path of the righteous, do not adhere to their plea, do not harken to their passionate polemic, to their persuasive eloquent propaganda. Be not a party to their group that councils treachery, that continues wickedness, that entertains constant plotting against the righteous and those that seek the straight path toward becoming upward in stature and steadfast in character. Thus man must always be aware of these external forces and internal pressures that surround hi mand sweep down upon him to uproot him from the path of progress. The character of the monarchy which has been amply discussed was brilliant in its external character though filled with chaos in its internal development. The temporary moment of tranquility was a moment of transition within the turmoil of Israel's political history.

After Solomon, as we know, the Judean empire was disected into two parts. Insurrection was the key note of the political establishment. Rebellion and revolt was the essence of its kingly dynasty. Only momentary religious revolutions created by Elijah on Mount Carmel and yehoyawdaw the kohain which provided monetary adjustment in the fiscal policy of Judah were expressions and experiences of sublime spiritual exalted moments in the period of this crucial politics that engulfed Israel. Israel begins to decay from its oral depravity. They enter into unholy alliances and involve themselves in the constant preoccupation of powerful military self-glorification. The crucial disaster, the event of despair occurred in 586 BCE. The Temple of G-d was torn down and the glory of Israel was stripped away when they were sent into captivity and exiled into Babylonia. For seventy years they would reside there until the appointed time would arrive when Almighty G-d would once again make His rendezvous; with the community of Israel, His chosen people. Not forever shall they be forsaken, not forever shall they be forlorn. The continuity of Israel, though interrupted with millenia of misery, centuries of misfortune, periods of tragedy, and ages of torment has always maintained its collective dignity and expression of unity in its most awesome moments of historical encounter. "For one fleeting moment have I left you," declares the prophet, "and with great mercy, compassion and feeling, shall I restore your glory and Israel will return to its homeland and rejuvenate itself on its promised land." The prophets sounded the constant vigil that Israel should be alerted to the fact that the Temple of G-d will not save them, nor will the dwelling place of the Almighty contain the armies of Babylonia. However, Almighty G-d declares to Jeremiah that he should buy plots of land and tracts of soil in Israel. For although destruction was foretold and disaster was inevitable, nevertheless hope will reawaken and restore Israel to its original glory. "For thy salvation had I hoped Oh G-d," declares Jacob. This is a vital and delightful instrument in the character of Israel. In time of darkened distress signals it plays a melodious tune that awakens the heart when all is asleep and silence overwhelms as a tardaymah—a deep slumber engulfs Israel, they cannot awaken from the nightfall of misery, they cannot extricate themselves from the plight of the dense darkness that has ascended upon them. Nevertheless, the prophet, Jeremiah who is filled with a sense of amazement and is awe-stricken at the contradictory prophetic experience that he has envisaged declares, "how can it be Oh G-d, because you have clearly defined Israel's destruction, how then should I buy plots of land, acres of agriculture growth?" "No," answers G-d, Israel though stricken for a moment in temporary anguish shall once again be able to realize and fulfill its everlasting timeless mission, its continuous heroic, histiric heritage for timeless humanity." The prophet conveys to Israel his message in an illustrious, metaphorical, heavenly muse.

The terms that he uses are eloquent in style and elegant in form Masaw dvar Hashem. The nuvee prophet proclaims the message of G-d's words. This term masaw is semantically identified with traveling masaw and masay are alike in sound and convey a similarity in content. The message of the prophet is to arouse the people from their lethargy and make them aware and concerned of their ethical character and moral behavior. The prophet comes to Israel with a definite mission to uplift and extricate the people of Israel and the nations of the universe from the plight of material enslavement, from the darkness of spiritual despair. The prophet is to motivate and guide, direct and instruct everyone in the path of spiritual uprightness, on the travel through life, on the historical travail through the trail of man's destiny. There are many varied encounters that he must confront, many challenges to battle, many conflicts to weather, many obstacles to overstep, many barriers to overcome. The message of the prophet therefore is to alleviate the plight of misery and convey the responsibility for spiritual concern and moral correctness. Therefore the prophet's message carries with it an onus, a responsibility, a burden and a yoke to shake the people from the shackles of spiritual depravity, to uproot them from their self-complacent attitude, to uproot them from the self-righteous contentment and smug feelings, for people find it easy to wrap themselves and cloak themselves in the material splendor and magnificence of enjoying the plush life. The majestic and sublime motif of the prophet is to evolve a spiritual and dynamic movement in the cultural development of both the particular Israel community and the general universal community.

Habain yakalee Efrayim eem yeled shaashooim kee meeday dabree vo sawchor eskorenoo od al kain humoo mayei lo noom ha shem—the prophet likens Efrayim to a child of delight unto G-d. The prophet equates Efrayim with a naive little boy who is the instrument of playful recreation for his creator. Why does the prophet associate Efrayim with the playful child? What is the significance within the content of Ephraim's mobility, Ephraim's princely regal pride and monarchal glory to be defined as a yeled shaashooim? Ephraim denotes the ability to be fruitful in conflict, productive in confrontation and a sign of singular exemplar character in challenge. Therefore, Ephraim which denotes the ability of expression and advancement is depicted and described as the child, "Katnos hamaychim" is the Kabbalistic metaphor that declares the naive creative curiosity of developing and forming intellectual creative principles to guide one along the path of spiritual progress. Ephraim is aptly characterized as the child who has not yet matured, not yet ripened, not yet completed her fruit. For in completion there is failure, in ripening there is decay. Ephraim is always in a state of growth always developing, always creating new concepts, new principles, it's dynamic in its content, brilliant in form, majestic in nature, eloquent in scope.

Amos, who rebelled against the repressive intolerant attitude of Amotziah expressed his defiance when he declares, "lo nuvee awnoochee vlo ben nuvee, kee boker ahnee oo vols shikmim"—I am a Sycamore cutter not a nuvee-prophet, not a man of great illustrious character, not a man of aristocracy; no, I am a purely Nomadic herdsman with no distinction of refined elevated stature. Amos, the prophet, realizes himself he must grow and develop with a spark of spiritual spontaneity if he is to mount the summit of attaining the spiritual plateau toward G-dliness.

David likewise was mcharker bchol oz—danced with all his strength and utilized all his energy to advance his sublime moral courage to the people, expressing his delight that the ark of the L-rd had been recovered and Israel's eternal brilliance had acquired a new rejuvenating spirit. Michal reprimanded him, she was sophisticated in her pride and her aristocratic behavior led her to reprove and admonish David for his rude and common behavior. The prophet continues that Michal had no children, expressing this note of deficiency in her character because she was so sophisticated and proud in her behavior that it incurred a distinctive mark of decay in her attitude toward G-d. She was smug in her relationship to G-d, overcome with a deep sense of self-satisfaction, with a self contented glow of self-righteous piety. David could be filled with inspiration and overwhelmed with a sense of poetic joy unto G-d, because he was always searching, never content with his present spiritual posture. Rather he was always cognizant of the fact that he must continually strive, always endeavor to become a more upright person, a higher ethical and moral being. Israel's preexilic universal character was quite discernable and recognizable for all the nations. When Yonadov extended kindness to Israel and concern for its anguish and grief, G-d promised that the house of Yonadov would be amply regarded and greatly honored. When the Gibeonites were slain by Saul, G-d brought a famine on the land and David had to pay retribution by hanging Saul's son as a token of concern for the Gibeonites, as a symbol of Israel's responsibility for shedding innocent blood. Thus the nations of the world were directly involved in Israel's heroic cultural destiny. Israel's historic heritage was demonstrated with convincing glory and immense courage.

Now in exile Israel's universal character assumed quite a different shape. Israel will be confronted with great challenges, immense trials, and terrifying tribulations. Israel's pages of historical travail begins to unfold. The arena of agony begins and the stage is set for Israel's existential drama. It is a historic portrayal wherein a nation has survived amidst stress and strife, not to be submerged in the sea of persecution, nor to be drowned in the ocean of despair, or to be overcome in the tidal wave of tyrannical persecution, and plunder, ravaged and ruined by its neighboring nations. The anti-semitic jealousy and anti-Israeli prejudice begins to take shape and a new picture is drawn. Israel will now have to preserve its destiny amidst an environment that is hostile to its heritage. The Samaritans tried to sabotage their attempts to rebuild and reestablish the firm security of Jerusalem and all of Israel. Ezrah and Nehemiah have to engage in the intellectual and physical battle against these neighbors who seek to assimilate from within and conquer from without the Jewish heritage. Now Israel must experience a new relationship, a varied association with the universal world community. Israel must experience a new challenge that will take it through the millenia of medieval triumph and tragedy. Ultimately, the community of Israel shall prevail. However it must endure immense struggle and suffer a titanic wave of tears. The post-exilic literature canonized in the Sacred Scripture sheds some light upon the new voyage of Israel. Esther and Daniel reflect the world arena, where Israel now must portray its everlasting timeless quality, its unique heroic heritage on the battle ground of cultural and spiritual warfare. Daniel is exposed to martyrdom. Shadrak, Mishak and Abednego are confronted with the challenge of surrendering their lives. This is a symbol of one's personal dedication on the sacred altar of Judaism. They express a defiance to power, they don't bow down to any idols nor convey their prayer to any other except the Almighty G-d. They are miraculously saved and redeemed from the perid and plight with which evil men wish to subdue and conquer them. We observe here that Daniel and Shadrack are subjugated to their own personal strife. It's an individual battle on a great intellectual creative scene where the officers or leaders of Israel are pitched in battle against the leaders of Persia and Babylonia. On a highly individualistic level Daniel and Shadrack confront their adversary and overcome the obstacle that is placed before them to entrap them. However in Esther the wicked Haman not only plots to murder Mordechai, his vicious conniving plan is to annihilate and exterminate the entire Jewish community. His aim is not only for the individual genius. He wishes to uproot the entire national collective genius of Judea. Not only for Mordechai does he declare his abuse, he reviles the entire Jewish community. Thus Israel is also miraculously saved. The redemptive quality of Israel is a rejuvenating factor that can never be blotted out. However dark the despair, however gloomy it appears, Israel shall forever prevail and maintain its continuity to convey its message for timeless humanity. We contrast the heroic martyrdom of Daniel with the classic intervention and overwhelming power of Esther. In Daniel we merely observe that they were extricated from the plight of bondage, from Esther we observe an emergence of a heroic community. Both are necessary and compliment each other; individual genius and quality of a person flows out and is a necessary concomittant from the national collective genius. They are inextricably intertwined and an integral part of one another. They are mutually indispensable and must coexist with each other. Esther denotes the historic triumphant battle of Israel against its foes, against its adversaries and enemies that wish to annihilate it and eradicate it from the face of the earth. Israel, however shall emerge victorious. We shall prevail. Esther communicates her wish, her plea for saving and redeeming her people when she exposes herself unto Achashverush. She must make an advance toward the universal world community. She is involved with her own anguish because she must go out and express her will to survive although she will experience suffering that she will be lost to the Jewish community. "Kasher avaditee awvauditee," she declared that she would be lost forever from the Jewish community. This redemptive feeling of martyrdom is a true example of Esther's unique character. She portrays the heroic Jewess that is willing to strip herself from her divine spark of holiness and expose herself to Achashverush, beguiling him and revealing herself to redeem Israel from the ensuing peril that has overwhelmed it. Esther comes forth and moves toward Achashverush to meet the enemy on his own terms, to strip Haman of his glory, to uproot the adversary that wishes to overtake Israel. In prior times before the exile had arrived Israel's universal contribution was quite distinct. Ruth went from the universal community to embrace Judaism. Ruth extricated herself from the world abominations of her heathen surroundings and her materialistic environment to involve herself in the Jewish spiritual and cultural development. She was enamored with the Jewish experience and her identity was only with the Jewish community. "My people are your people, my G-d is your G-d," declared Ruth. Wherever you lodge, shall I lodge, is her sincere wish and genuine desire. Ruth and Esther reflect the ever prevalent duality of Israel's relationship with the universal community. At times the Israelite community accepts and receives the universal general community with open arms, with a willingness that they may also experience the glory of Almighty G-d, that they also should be accepted under the wings of His spiritual guidance and protective paternal fate and faith. However Esther reflects the serious and sensitive suffering that the Jew has to overcome in time of torment, in age of strife, in period of turmoil. Israel must confront the enemy on the battleground. The rabim mayamay haaretz misyahadim. After the redemptive, supernatural, miraculous intervention of G-d on behalf of Israel had occurred, the nations of the world were over-awed with the majestic awesome power of G-d. They assumed a religious experience, their character was transformed into a transcending element in attaining the sublime spiritual oneness of G-d. The mission of Israel is not merely to isolate itself and become segregated from the world community. This was never the aim delegated to Israel nor was it its concern to be smug and self-complacent with its own self-righteous and contented attitude that it alone is regarded with the blissful religious experience of being G-d's exalted people. "Vaal yomar ben hanaychur hanilvaw el ha shem havdail hivdeelanee ha shem maya amo" declares Isaiah. Let not the stranger express his despair that he has become separated and aloof from G-d because he is not a member of the Israelite community. He has also a share in the cultural, spiritual and blissful regard of cleaving unto G-d. Thus in Jonah we experience G-d's care, concern, and compassion for the nations of the world. Nineveh should not become obliterated because of her transgressions. She must also have the opportunity to repent, she must also experience a sense of reawakening. Perhaps she can extricate herself from the plight of her spiritual pitfall, perhaps she can elevate herself from the depths of moral decay. Therefore Jonah is compelled by the will of G-d to go and prophetize on Nineveh that her doom is imminent because there may yet arise within her community, she may yet become overwhelmed with the sense of G-dliness and thus return to G-d. The road to spiritual commitment is not blocked off to those who have transgressed. G-d intervenes even for the heathern. G-d stretches out His hand to pluck those who have descended into the abyss of moral and spiritual decay. He extends His mighty hand of kindness to all. Therefore, Jonah who is reluctant to express his message of penitence and warning of doom to

Nineveh must reconcile his contention and transform his will to the obedience of G-d's commandment. Honah perhaps would have been content if Nineveh would repent on her own. He perhaps entertained a passive religious view for the heathen. If they observe the light of G-d on their own, then they too would have an equal share and participate in the glory of G-d. However, Jonah was not involved actively in participating in Nineveh's resurrection and rejuvenation from the despair of her moral and spiritual decadence. Jonah was not eager or anxious to uplift and extricate Nineveh from her pitfall and plight of spiritual abyss. Thus, He was reluctant and fled from G-d as it were for he was unwilling to prophetize on Nineveh. He was not involved or concerned with the universal world community. The answer of G-d is, "I am concerned." Ayekaw G-d asks Adam. G-d asks Kayin where are you, where is Hevel, your brother? G-d is concerned and involved with the world, with the plight of its spiritual decay. G-d cannot dissociate, disengage himself from the world community or from the particular Israelite community. Periodically in history we have seen great strife and stress, tragedy and torment. However, ultimately history shall prevail on the national and international level, on the universal and particular for G-d's grace and glow shall forever reign supreme and sovereign. This is the message to Jonah. The mission of Israel to the world is that she must declare whether actively or passively her willingness to convey and communicate, transmit its tenets of faith and creeds of tradition to transform the world and her own community, to elevate themselves in attaining the sublime spiritual message, the unique historic heritage when all will be fused in a unique blissful oneness to serve G-d, to experience His glory, to be enamorad in His wonder. That we shall experience that day when we can leeros mhayraw bsiferes oozechaw—to see the luster of Thy strength, the glamor of Thy glory that all the nations of the world will accept and admire, respect and revere the name of G-d. Vhawyaw hashem lmelech al kul haaretz byom hahoo yeeyeh hashem echud ooshmo echud—on that day the name of G-d sall be exalted and magnified for all mankind.

ON THE HOLIDAYS

Chapter 6

The three festivals of Israel's pilgrimage to Jerusalem: Passover, Feast of Weeks, and Tabernacles are all concerned with one unique element, the consecration of time and nature within the context of nature. The agricultural produce of a people is not to be abused beyond religious or spiritual enjoyment. A country's material abundance, economic affluence must be sublimated and transcended to achieve the ultimate identification and cleaving to G-d. Now let us explain the interconnection and interrelationship between Passover, Shavuous and Succos. They are all bound up with a unique brachah—blessing—that G-d has sanctified the smanim—periodic festivals—with his nation Israel. Nature is not a phenomenon beyond the scope of mankind. It must be sublimated and transformed to serve the will of man, that he may grow and develop in his cultural and spiritual dedication unto G-d. Shavuous is the festival of Torah wherein we celebrate the giving of the Torah on Mount Sinai and the first fruits that man offers—chag habikoorim to the Temple. Thus the *Genesis* of Israel's creative culture is uniquely blended with the *Genesis* of man's productive agricultural work. This creative work must be inextricably intertwined with the agricultural or material splendor in which he is engaged. His activities on the material level, on the economic plane, are not isolated phenomenon nor are they to be segregated from the intellectual creative experience of Israel. Rather they must be synthesied and interwoven with one another. Succos represents the festival of peace, the solemn, sacred, spiritual, blissful relationship with G-d and mankind that Israel shall attain. The seventy cows, bullocks represent the seventy nations for which Israel is morally responsible and ethically obligated in conveying the mission of G-d, in communicating His words to them. Thus, haporais sookas shalom—spreading the peaceful Tabernacle is the sublime aim and spiritual motif of Succos. Peace is the symbol of this holiday that transcends all of man's lustful drive and unquenchable thirst to gain power, acquire territory, extend boundaries beyond his geographical locations, beyond his borders. Succos declares for all mankind the aim of peace, the motif of serenity. This universal declaration of peace is amply described in Zokariah wherein all the nations of the world shall be punished if they do not ascend to the mountain of Zion on this holiday in declaring their ambition and supreme aim in fostering peace, in developing a spiritual serenity. Pesach is symbolically identified with freedom, the extrication of Israel from the plight of bondage, from the inhumane suffering of servitude, of becoming morally depraved in an asphyxiating environment that engulfs and strangles man's ability to advance himself and become creative. Thus, the prophet declares, "vawareh osuch misbosesses bdam vomar bdomayich hahee bdomayich hahee—by your blood you shall exist, by your blood you shall convey the message of the existential drama of Israel." That freedom must be achieved even at the cost of incurring martyrdom. Thus the Torah that is celebrated on Shavuous is the pivotal structure of Pesach and Succos. Pesach is freedom, Succos is peace; both are inextricably intertwined, both are dependent upon the Torah. Without the Torah there is no peace nor is there freedom.

Within this context we can conceive of scheeros—six passages wherein the Torah has specifically commanded us to remember, that it should be an indelible imprint upon our souls for our timeless historical destiny, for our creative national genius. We must remember, be ever alert, ever diligent to maintain the ever present vigil of remembering and preserving our great culture. Remember what G-d has commanded you on Mount Horeb, lest you should forget and lest you shall dismiss them (the precepts) from your heart. Remember the Sabbath and sanctify it. Remember the *Exodus* where G-d delivered you from the seat of bondage, from the yoke of oppression. Remember what G-d did to Miriam. Remember how you angered G-d when you disobeyed His utterance, when you fashioned a golden calf, idol worship, which I have expressly forbidden. Remember what G-d did to Amalek who tried to ensnare you in the pitfall of military subjugation. When you were tired and weary Amalek tried to overwhelm you and overpower you.

What do these passages, commandments of memory wish to convey? The Torah is the pivotal structure of Shabbas and yitseeas mitzrayi. Shabbos which is the sine qua non of peace, yitseeas mitzrayim, the ultimate goal of freedom. Therefore, G-d tells us to remember the positive aim of Torah balanced by peace and freedom. Remember also the negative declaration against this aim. Miriam tried to uproot the unique sanctity of the Mosaic creed when she spoke evil against Moses. Remembrance of the aygel—golden calf—is a warning against sliding into the pitfall of spiritual decay and moral abyss, because the aygel symbolizes the god of Egypt from whom Almighty G-d had extricated Israel. Remember Amalek who tried to wage war against you, who was plotting to uproot your peaceful religious existence and spiritual blissful cohesiveness. Thus, in memory of G-d's precept and the act of the festival the activity of the pilgrimage are inextricably intertwined with one another. Both the memory of the mind with the acting of man's material cumulative success are necessary, both are indispensable in attaining the summit of G-d's spiritual plateau.

Rosh Hashannah, the supreme holy New Year, is ushered in by the sacred and awesome Holy Day. The liturgy is eloquent in character, elegant in scope. What do we pray for? What is the essential characteristic of the musaf prayer that is the pinnacle apex for our spiritual outpouring unto G-d? What is the intrinsic concept wherein we underscore our religious conviction unto G-d? The prayer on Rosh Hashonah is the realization of Israel's sacred sovereign spiritual mission within a context of a universal community that will enjoy the fruits become enriched by the intellectual creativity and spiritual productivity of Israel's unique historic heritage. Oovchain tain pachdechaw—Almighty G-d convey Thy awesome majestic reverence upon the nations of the world that everyone should come and prostrate himself before your glory, before your grandeur. The nations of the world shall realize their creative fulfillment in one unique covenant, in a unified spiritual oneness that will express Thy glory and accentuate the influence of G-d's grace. Therefore G-d grant glory to the nation, praise to those who revere thee, joy to your land which you have chosen to express and convey the covenantal mission of G-dliness. Then shall G-d reign with glory, on the Mountain of Zion in the city of Jerusalem. G-d is sanctified in a passive manner, Hawel Ha kadosh mikdash btzdakah let Almighty G-d reign forever, let His grace endure for timeless humanity. The prayer concludes with this sanctification of G-d's name in a passive manner. The next blessing introduces G-d's grandeur and His great glory in an active, moving, dynamic, creative manner. Malcheeos—we hope and aspire that all the nations shall accept by their own cognition and by their own free will Thy glory. Thy grandeur shall reign abundantly with the immense magnificence and the intensive splendor that is so attractive to all. The malchoos—kingdom of G-d shall be acknowledged in an active creative manner. Men shall come and nations shall come to the realization that Hashem Elohay Yisroel Melech oo malchoose bkolmashawlaw—all men, all creatures of G-d shall realize that Almighty G-d is the Supreme, sovereign mover in the historic drama of mankind-vomar kulasher nshawmaw veeapo—and all shall come to acknowledge, everyone that has a breath in his soul will express the idea and realize that the G-d of Israel is the king and His sovereignty reigns throughout the entire universe. This blessing of zichronos underscores again the national historic mission to convey to the universal world community the idea of creative sacred spirituality. Upon the countries of the world it shall be proclaimed which one is to the sword, which one is to peace, which one shall enjoy economic splendor and material gain, which one shall encounter depression and recession. Also Noah in the Ark you have remembered with Your great glory and kindness to redeem him from the deluge. When man displayed his disobedience unto G-d then the Almighty One was filled with fury against the universal community. However the memory of Noah's kindness and acts of righteousness graced their way before G-d so that He may confer His benevolence upon mankind and restore the universal community with the brith hakeshes—the covenant of the rainbow. No deluge shall destroy mankind, no torrent rainfall shall annihilate the world-wide community. Then G-d remembers His specific unique covenant with His chosen, selected, elite group, the Patriarchs that represent Israel's heroic mission and holy message to the nations of the world. Moreover, G-d declares that he shall even remember the Promised Land from where Israel has been driven forth to the Diaspora, dispersed and disgruntled. Therefore G-d shall remember the covenant of old with your forefathers. The promise unto Abraham, Isaac, and Jacob shall not remain devoid of fulfillment. The blessing concluded G-d remembers the covenant of the rainbow of the universal community and the particular covenant with the community of Israel representing the blessing of Israel's acceptance of the great tenets of our tradition and principles of our faith. The classic drama was a magnificent scene of splendor as G-d conveyed the Torah on Mount Sinai and communicated His ordinances unto Moses. Then in the midst of the blessing kol hanshumu thalall yah—all the souls, everyone who possesses a spirit within his soul shall sing with joy, proclaim with homage of G-d's grace and His grandeur. Shofur—shoofraw in Aramaic—represents the beauty of Israel, consecration and dedication of Israel is sublime, spiritual, economic, material and cultural sacrifice unto G-d. Thus the prayer of Rosh Hashana is exuding with G-d's grace to Israel and the nations of the world. G-d is bound up with Israel and the Noachite community. Avraham and Hoach with brith, chesid and shevooah—covenant, grace and oath. Covenant is a mutual relationship, both are equal partners. Chesed denotes the idea of G-d conveying an extra abundant share beyond His required legal obligation. Shevooah declares G-d that although Israel is not worthy, the world is guilty, nevertheless we bind G-d with an oath that the world shall continue, that His glory may be proclaimed throughout the world.

In Adam shatah bhaimaw ma chatah—The law states that

if a man commits sodomy with an animal then the animal must also be slain. Why so? Because the animal kingdom, the plant kingdom and the universe have been created to serve mankind wherein man should sublimate the nature of the world so he may realize and fulfill the Divine message wherein he may ascend to the spiritual summit and celestial heights of the glorious and majestic presence of the shechinah, of the Divine spirit. Thus the din of Rosh Hashanah wherein all mankind passes before Almighty G-d who decrees His judgment and declares His decision. We express the hope and acknowledge that our firm desire is the realization of His majestic glory and noble grandeur throughout the entire universe. Now, Rosh Hashanah ushers; in the New Year with magnificent awe and awesome splendor. The ten day penitential period culminates in the solemn, celestial, sacred Day of Atonement. Kaitz mcheelaw sleechaw, the day of purification, of self-scrutiny, self-investigation, and personal exploration is the moment when G-d's encounter with the community of Israel and the universal world body is one of forgiveness and compassion. We read the classic story of Jonah, where Nineveh was spared, its inhabitants were saved from the awesome danger of moral decay and spiritual corrosion. I should have mercy on Nineveh for G-d's true message in compassion and concern for those who are humble in spirit and contrite in soul, Yom Kippur, that day of forgiveness, that moment when Satan has no ability to cast his evil and malicious oratory and polemics against the world, against mankind, against civilization is a day when the din of Rosh Hashanah culminates in rachamim, when law and justice are blended together, when the normative structure of society is placed against the background of compassion and within the reference of concern.

Moses commanded the Jews with many laws, many norms, many regulations. There are few case law proceedings that have been reported in the *Bible*. Four cases problems illustrate the *Bible*'s dual concern for justice and law, for order and peace. The mkoshesh aitzim—the chopper of wood on the Sabbath was executed; the one who cursed G-d, who uttered blasphemous words against the Almighty was also convicted with the death penalty. However when those who were contaminated because they had been occupied with burial procedures came to Moses with the plea that they will not share in the Pascal sacrifice, they will not have the right to participate in the communal offering of freedom, Moses asked G-d and the answer was conveyed to him that another Pesach, another day will be selected for those who cannot bring the offering on the regular day of Nisan. They shall have another opportunity wherein they may also fulfill the obligation and have equal participation in the communal sacrifice of freedom. The daughters of Tzeluvchud complained to Moses that they will not have any share in the land, they were not bequeathed with a portion in the land because their father, they declared, left no male issue. G-d answers them with his concern for all humanity that kain duvros bnos Tzeluvchud—they are right in their argument, they are correct in the contention, they must also have an equal share in the inheritance, an equal portion in the promised land to come. Thus the questions raised to Moses express a concern for law and a sympathetic understanding for mankind.

Yom Kippur is also the day when we ask forgiveness for the atrocities that have been committed, for the negligence of man's apathy and his lack of responsibility shunning the yoke of moral concern. There are two reasons given for the Day of Atonement, why Israel was compelled to offer a fast: (1) Atonement for the sin of the golden calf, (2) we offer our confession, we express our sympathy, we expect G-d's forgiveness because of our lack of responsibility when the brethren sold Joseph into slavery. The jealousy of the brothers who were not aware of Joseph, they were not eager to hear him out with dignity or respect. Hamashel timshel banuhamalech timloch alaynoo, will thou rule over us, overwhelmed with greed against the ingenius creativity of Joseph. Yom kippur is the expression of Man's concern for his intellectual creative goals and for his productive material aspiration. Both are indispensible and mutually interdependent for making and developing toward a greater society and a more harmonius community. The Rosh Hashanah liturgy expresses another remarkable concept infusing and blending the particular community with the universal world body. "Zeh hayom tcheelas maasechaw zeekawron lyom reeshon," declares the liturgy. This is the day when thy creation has commenced a memory for that first day. The history of world creation—hayom haras olam—the birthday of humanity is recorded on this High Holy Day. The solemn awesome event of man's account of his doings and all his deeds are placed, as it were, before the Almighty. This is the character of zichronos, of memory, reminding man of his duty and obligation, his moral responsibility and social concern for the world, for the history of creation, for the history of nature.

Basaurah mamoros nivrah haolum—In ten utterances, in ten dicta was the world created. Then the blessing of shafros, teh prayer of the trumpet pronouncement depicts and describes the epoch making eventful moment of mamod Har Sinai, when Israel stood before Almighty G-d on the mountain of Sinai to accept the Torah, to obey His commandments, to understand and study the intellectual creative concepts and precepts of Almighty G-d. The aseres hadibros therefore are blended and merged with the asawuaw mamoros. Ten utterances of G-d denote the history of creation. Ten precepts of G-d to his nation convey the message how humanity should behave, how Israel should communicate her tenets of faith and principles of tradition to civilization at large. Therefore, the psalmist proclaims in his prayer ha shamayim msaprim kvod el covnasay yawduv magid hawrawkeeah.

The heavens of the world, the galaxies of the universe, the milky way and the moon all declare and sing the heavenly muse of G-d's miraculous and wonderful creation. Vayn nistur maychamawso—nothing is concealed from the bright and burning sun, from the gala glamor, from the historic glitter of world creation. This is not an isolated phenomena however; this does not grow in a vacuum; nature is not a mere splendor of G-d, it is wrapped with the garments of intellectual glow of creative glitter, of Toras ha shem temeemah, meesheevas nefesh, the word, of G-d. His Torah is perfect and complete refreshing the soul. His commandments are true, all of them combined express the supreme task to mold a righteous community. We note also the classic statement in the pirke avoth, he who is engrossed in learning and departs from his study to become enamored with nature and overwhelmed with the miraculous wonder of the great majestic beauty of world civilization is guilty with his life. He is responsible for the supreme penalty. We may insert this observation, the Mishnah expressly utilizes the term haporaish meemishawso—about one who departs from his course of study to glance at nature, to observe its beauty and wonder. Nature is not to be separated and to be made a distinctive entity from one's course of study. We must integrate nature and sublimate it to make man a transcendent being, to enhance our lives, to advance our spiritual and cultural growth. This is the object of the majestic beauty and the divine glory of nature. veseekin hawyoo gomrim osaw im hanaytz hachamaw—Those who are zealous in their spiritual adherence and religious commitment used to wake up when the sun rays began to gleam. When the ray of sun was seen across the horizon, they would stand and pray to unify nature with prayer. Thus Rosh Hashanah, the solemn day of the New Year is the occasion when Israel unifies and formulates its harmonious law into a blissful spiritual, integrated whole, with natures' majestic beauty and magnificent glory.

Hashem pakades Sarah kasherawmar—G-d had visited Sarah as he originally declared that Kayschayaw ool Sarah bain—that the child of Sarah shall have continuity, not only spiritually, also biologically. Sarah shall reap the fruits of her intellectual creativity and spiritual productivity, she will bear fruit for future generations Naitzer matawei masay yawdei lhispawayr—branches of my tree to extol the virtues of G-d, to express the glory of the Almighty One. Why does Sarah request to have children? What is the reason, what is the drive for Sarah to have children? Naturally every woman would like to have recognition, would like to express her ambition in a self-fulfilling prophecy of her children for timeless humanity. Rachel complains to Jacob provide for me children if not, then there is no reason for my living. The classic prayer of Hannah expressing G-d's great, miraculous, intervention to give her issue that she may also sprout forth biologically, that she may enjoy the productivity of her fruits. Rosh Hashanah wherein we read this chapter where G-d consoles, and considers Sarah with his compassion for her on this awesome magnificent day of splendor there is a heroic encounter where G-d confronts man in a rendezvous to uplift and extricate him from the plight of spiritual decay, from the abyss of moral depravity and G-d answers that yes, there is continuity, there is a historic, heroic, heritage, there is a unique message to convey, a specific mission to communicate. The tenets of my faith must be expressed, a faith in G-d of declaring His glory, glamor and grace throughout the entire world community. This is Samuel of whom Chana declared that he will be devoted unto G-d, destined to perform the heroic duty of Israel's historic heritage, to issue judgments, to declare verdicts for the people. Thus the power of woman to have children to propagate, is not a lustful drive; it is not predicated on greed, on pride, no, it is an expression of G-d's glory, a declaration that this creative work is an ongoing developing process for the everlasting timeless world community and His particular privileged community of Israel.

A note now on Purim. What is this joyous, what is this glorious occasion, what significance do we attribute to this miraculous battle wherein Judea encountered the forces of Anti-Semitism, that seek to annihilate and eradicate her, that prey upon the moral apathy and spiritual laxity of Israel? However in time of strife, in period of torment, Israel gathers herself together—Laich kanos es kol hayehoodim—Go and call an assembly for all the Jews, no class distinction, no party separation, we are all one, ready to combat the enemy that seeks to destroy, that preys upon the apparent weakness of humility. No, Israel declares to the world that the secular world, the commercialized community, the materialized structure of the mundane society, is to be synthesized and blended in a unique, harmonious, oneness with our spiritual blissful religious existence, Israel therefore declares to the world that Ishtar and Marduk are transformed and the symbols of secular deities sublimated to Mordechai and Esther. G-d is concealed in the paradox of human anomaly. Removed and remote He stands at a great distance. Mayrachok neeraw aylei hashem—far off, from a great distance G-d has appeared to me. This concealed manner of G-d is not always removed, nor will it ever become severed from the community of Israel. The Megillah therefore is called a sayfer and an eegeres.

It is a book to communicate the tenets of our faith and the principles of our tradition to the world at large. However, we must realize our own commitment and fulfill our own historic obligation reconciling our own identity with the larger broader community. We operate on two levels and our battleground consists of two flanks, namely, blending and synthesizing the secular with the sacred. There is no division, no diversity, no disparity between the two. They are integrated in the text context of keedooshah graduation of sanctity and processes of holiness. Eegeret—letter however is a private personalized letter wherein our own strategy, our own ethical principles have to be molded and developed, shaped and formed, wherein we will be able to communicate and convey these ideas, these messages, and this great holy mission to the world wide community. Megillah is semantically termed galoh—closing and opening, revealing and concealing. This is the process of man's prescription in engaging with the world, in expressing the glory of G-d, in enhancing and advancing the great moral ethic, the soonum bonum the ultimate goodness, the divine providence of hashras hashechina and hashpaas hakedooshah of Almighty G-d.

Esther is the expression of proving the ways of the world and sublimating them, that we may transcend our personal ethical being and elevate ourselves to the spiritual plateau, where the entire world shall recognize the celestial beauty and majestic reverence of Almighty G-d. This is the blueprint of Torah shebaalpeh. Esther is the last of the miraculous deeds that have been written down for the ages, that have been canonized in scribal sanctity. Chanukah on the other hand, cannot be written is not subject to be expressed within the context of the sacred canon law of the Holy Scripture. Chanukah is distinct and different. It is the great long battle, where we kindle the festival of lights to illuminate Israel throughout the dense darkness of despair, throughout the long arduous night of medieval millenia. This is how Israel shall console herself in time of strife, in period of stress, in age of torment throughout the great frustrating, historic heroic night before the dawn of glory will arise, before the sun of G-d's splendor shall glitter across the horizon. There is a long arduous night, a great long conquest that can only be liberated within the context of law and order, against the background of justice and humanitarian acts, and within the framework of compassion and concern. Therein lies Israel's welfare, tranquility, and security. This is the idea of Chanukah, this is how we strive and aspire for a celestial, blissful, peaceful, religious community. Therefore, G-d, answers Job from the thunderlap of the great tempestuous storm and declares, hayawdata, canst thou know, are thow knowldegeable of my workings, of my great supervision? Do you have the knowledge and understanding? Can you fathom my works? Mee madad bashamayim —who can measure the heaven and the earth, and the entire universe, celestial, special spheres, who can ascend to the great heights of G-d? To His infinite knowledge, man is but a finite, qualified limited structure. From the stress and storm of Israel's heroic historic destiny, from the age of torment and the period of turmoil throughout the long, harried night there lies a glorious glow wherein G-d's name will be hallowed for historic, timeless humanity. The persecution and agonies of Job reflect the universal national process wherein communities of Israel were ravaged and ruined, pillaged and plundered, and yet Israel shall forever remain and maintain her historic mission.

The measurements of the Aron, the Ark of the L-rd were fragmentary and designated in fractionary terms to delineate the concept that for all our learning, all our study, we stand only at the beginning, at the aleph, for all man's travail and toil on the earth he is only at the aleph of understanding the threshold of knowledge, the hayadata, can he conceive, can he know the Almighty One, the Infinite One? Only with a sensitive creative imagination do we aspire with all our limitations, with our quantified, finite, know-how to ascertain our evergrowing ever-burdening, ever-increasing dynamic thirst that is insatiably unquenchable for the knowledge of G-d.

Why do we read Ruth on Shevuoth? What is the symbolic significance of the story of Ruth that culminates in the narrative concluding in the genealogy leading up to King David.

What lesson can we derive in reading Ruth on the day that the Torah was given to Israel?

Moshe and David represent two great pillars in the development of cultural, creative Judias. Moshe represents the master of internal growth, development and commitment to the Jewish ideal. King David represents the architect of external glamour, glitter and glow of kingship. The Midrash declares zichroo toras Moshe avdi and Mizmoor sheer chanookas habayis lDovid. The Torah is designated unto Moshe and the Temple is dedicated unto David because these two great men sacrificed their lives and dedicated themselves for the purpose of establishing a permanent Judaism. Moses is the symbol and representative par excellence of the Torah—the cultural, the intellectual, spiritual development of the Torah. David is the symbol par excellence of bayis, of the House establishing a dwelling place for Israel; realizing secure boundaries for the Nation. Thus the Holy Temple, the House that symbolizes the external character of sanctity and the Torah which is the internal character of Judaism blend together and merge on Shevuoth in the reading of the Torah and the reading of Ruth. Go out and see the glory with which the King has been crowned. Byom chasenooso oovyom simchas leeba. On the day of his marriage, on the day of his heart's delight Byom chasenooso—the day of marriage—that's the day of matan Torah—giving of the Torah. The Mishnah comments: What's the day of gladdening and rejoicing of the heart. That is the Binyan Bais Hamikdosh, the establishment and construction of the Holy Temple. Bais Hamikdosh matan Tora represent the internal growth and external development of the Jewish Nation. This dual experience of Torah and Temple are realized in the lecturnal reading of Shevuoth. Also we must understand the parallel idea of Shevuoth wherein there is reference made in the Book of Jubilees that the Maabel (deluge) ceased and Noah's Ark came to rest on the day of Shevuoth. The oath that G-d made to Noah—kee maiNoach nishbaatee zohs—no more shall a flood ever consume mankind—was issued on Shevuoth. Therefore we have the particular Shevuoth of Mooshboyim V'ohmdim mhar sinai—that we have an obligation to fulfill, a mission to perform and roles to carry out—run parallel to the Shevuoth, to the general civilization, to the general culture of Shevuoth wherein G-d promised to Noah that the general and world civilization shall continue and endure. This is the message of Shevuoth. We would like to add a dictum from the Talmud, concerning Shevuoth. Everyone agrees, declares the Talmud, that ahtzeres which is Shevuoth is contingent upon our social participation in the enjoyment and realization of that holiday—in merrymaking on a social and familial level. Hakohl modeem bahtzeret debeenum lchem. Everyone concurs that Shevuoth is the idea of Torah sublimating the material drives and physical urge to an internally blissful, and intrinsically sublime religious experience.

Now a thought for Rosh Hashanah, the High Holy Days. We blow on Rosh Hashanah a tkeeaw and a troaah. Tkeeaw is a simple blast. Trooah is a blast which is broken up into several parts. Shevarim—a variation of trooah is likewise a fragmentary blast. Tkeeah is a simple, direct and complete blast. The tkeeah and the trooah have very deep philosophical connotations and a theological significance—that must be spelled out in these terms.

Tkeeah symbolizes a rather fixed and stable position in life of one who assumes a high prestigious position in the social stratum of his group life. Tawkah ohawlo—He fixed his tent, he established his dwelling place and made a permanent settlement. Trooah, on the other hand, is a fragmentary splitting broken aspect of life. It is filled with confrontation, conflict and challenge. The term trooah means breaking, shattering, splitting. Hence the tkeeah and the trooah symbolize two different positions and postures of social stratum. The tkeeah is the static, th trooah the dynamic aspect of one's religious aspirations, motivations developing the ultimate drive for the knowledge of G-d. There is a chavair and a raiah the type of person who binds, heals, and assists. On the other hand, there is a raiah—one who criticizes, complains and is irritated by the atrocities, transgressions and iniquities that persist and continue in the process of society. There are those people who are established—tkeeah. Their life is fully acknowledged—as the Rambam would declare—kav yawshur—no problems, no plight, no puzzles to overcome, to overstep and to overpower. However, there is another class of people who face challenges, confrontations and conflicts. Moshel broocho. There again, Ellul symbolizes on the one hand ahnee idodee vdodee lee. On the other hand it symbolizes eslvovchah ves lvav. Ahnee idodee means great friendship, the posture of pleasantness, comraderie, brotherhood, filial companionship with G-d. However es lvovchah symbolizes the cathartic process that man must undergo to rid himself of his material and mundane drives, to extricate himself from the plight of his dismal descent to the pitfall of his spiritual ensnarement. Es lvovchah, means the attempt to extricate oneself from the plight dilemma and complex problems that tend to engulf one in a sea of turmoil—to immerse one in an ocean of stress—to overwhelm one in a valley of terror. Thus to aspire and to assume a sublime spiritual plateau we have to acknowledge the polarity of es lvovchah and ahnee ldodee. Both ideas blend, merge and fuse to ignite the spark of the sacred devotion to G-d, to influence man, to encourage him on the long rugged road of cleaving unto G-d. The winding twisting curves in the road tend to ensnare him and entrap him that he may not be able to fulfill his mission and continue in the ongoing tradition and the timeless process of Torah—true Judaism. Rosh Hashanah, then, is a renewal, a rededication, a resolve to the understanding that we have to combine these elements of kav yawshor-moshel broocho, of tkeeah and trooah of chavair and raiah and of ahnee ldodee—es lvovchah. Both are needed; both are desirable. They complement one another, to accelerate and enhance and moreover to advance the goal of greater religious relationship and spiritual association with G-d. That is the message of Rosh Hashanah.

What is the significance that we may derive and that will consequently help us to develop our religious and spiritual character in the lesson of Jonah that we read on Yom Kippur? Jonah in the whale is caught up in the dilemma of the realization of one's particular environment and reconciling it with the universal environment. The question why Jonah fled from the will of G-d to prophetize is quite significant and indeed, merits some investigation. Why Jonah was caught up in the whale is also of paramount importance. Why the story of Jonah sets the scene in a style wherein Jonah has fallen asleep and he is not concerned. Moreover he is apathetic to the problem of those who are in distress at sea. Jonah is not involved in the plight of the turmoil of the tidal wave, of the onrushing tide that seeks to submerge the boat into oblivion. Why also is there no concern for Jonah to save Nineveh—the great city.

Perhaps they shall repent. Perhaps they shall turn from their trespass that they have committeed against G-d.

Jonah finally comes and recites his prophecy of peril that in 40 days Nineveh shall be overturned and made into a heap of rubble. There is an immediate transformation of feeling on behalf of the Ninivites. They are immediately overcome by the shattering expectations and tragic heralding of events. They repent and turn from the atrocities which they have committed. However Jonah originally conceived of a different notion that penitence, the grace of penitence of which Rabbeinu Jonah Gerondi describes as the chasdoh hagodol, of G-d's grace which he has bestowed upon Man the quest for penitence—to escape from the ensnarements that may trap him and to seek refuge within the context of aspiring to G-d is reserved only for Israel, his particular community. Jonah was of the opinion that with regard to the nations of the world they must come to penitence on their own accord and volition. We find two motifs of penitence. Shoovaw yisroel kee chawshaltaw banvonechaw. Return O Israel to your G-d because you have stumbled and failed in your drive, in your passion for the mundane, material splendor. There is another concept—Heenai awnochee mifateehaw vholachteehaw hamidbur. During the darkest moments of man's dismal descent to the abyss of the spiritual failures, G-d reaches out and uplifts him from his material mire. G-d will not let man slip and sink into that mire. Rather He calls to him and will extricate him from the horrors of his evils. And I will give, declares Ezehiel, a new heart, a new spirit to my people. Removing the heart of stone and replacing it with a heart of penitential feeling with emotion for the spiritual and sublime ideas of G-dliness. Jonah could not assume that this grace was bestowed upon goyim to that degree that G-d also, as it were, calls to humanity at large, to the entire world civilization in their darkest moments of distress to extricate and uplift them from the peril and misfortune of submerging into complete chaos from the catastrophic blunder of the idolatry of mankind, of man's idolatrous drive and the passion and pride for his material thirst and lust.

And G-d declares, "Jonah, you had pity on a gourd that in one night has come and in one night has evaporated and I shall not have mercy and compassion and consideration for Nineveh who has so many scores of thousands of people that will be cast away because of their sins. The message is clear that in time of strife and stress in an age of turmoil and torment the prophet calls with a clamor, addressing mankind to uproot himself from the slumber, to awaken himself from his lethargy.

Arise from your pitfall of spiritual failure. Therefore Jonah was submerged in the whale because the whale symbolizes the Nineveh cult—not to be isolated from the world civilization or assimilated by it. Rather to contribute to it. This is the idea of Jonah's prophecy that Jonah has a mission to convey the message of tshoovaw to the entire world civilization. Jonah cannot neither escape nor can he be swallowed up in the whole that symbolizes the culture of Nineveh. Rather the motif of Jonah is to liberate and to instruct the heathen both on the individual and on the communal level. We see an overwhelming transformation of the character of the Goy. The sailors on the ship and tourists on that boat brought offerings to G-d. They were overwhelmed by the majestic awe of G-d's grace, that in a split second they were to be drowned and then a moment later, the storm subsided and the ship was put to rest at port. And, likewise, Nineveh, the great community which was destined to doom and failure and destruction and to disappear from the face of the earth, discovered its true identity to see the light and the illuminating spark of G-d's grace and wisdom. Jonah is swallowed up by the whale because he wanted to isolate himself. We cannot isolate ourselves because isolation leads to annihilation. To convey the influence and to exert the spirit of Almighty God is the supreme message of Jonah—Hodoo ladoshem—declare amidst the nations G-d's great attributes.